IMAGES
of America

NEW YORK'S
LINERS

IMAGES
of America

NEW YORK'S
LINERS

John A. Fostik, MBA

ARCADIA
PUBLISHING

Published by Arcadia Publishing
Charleston, South Carolina

Library of Congress Control Number: 2014953450

For all general information, please contact Arcadia Publishing:
Telephone 843-853-2070
Fax 843-853-0044
E-mail sales@arcadiapublishing.com
For customer service and orders:
Toll-Free 1-888-313-2665

Visit us on the Internet at www.arcadiapublishing.com

*This book is dedicated to Diana, Melissa, Chris,
Jeff, Tim, and grandchildren Helena and Christina.
Like a ship has anchors, they are mine.*

CONTENTS

Acknowledgments   6

Introduction   7

1.   The Great Ocean Bridge   9

2.   Sea Giants of the Edwardian Era   17

3.   After the Great War   33

4.   Ships of State   43

5.   Sailing to Victory   55

6.   Postwar Liners   63

7.   A Sea Change from Crossings to Cruising   73

8.   Millennial Liners   95

9.   Memorabilia   115

10.   On the Horizon   125

ACKNOWLEDGMENTS

Special thanks go to my title manager at Arcadia Publishing, Sharon McAllister, for her advocacy and guidance. Thanks go to Bob Coolidge, to Ian Fried–New York Economic Development Corporation, to Tina Rossell–Royal Caribbean International, and especially to Byron Huart for use of photographs. Except where indicated, all photographs are from the author's collection.

INTRODUCTION

To understand the present-day Port of New York, it is helpful to recall its past. The credit for the discovery of the harbor in 1524 goes to the Florentine explorer Giovanni da Verrazano. As befits his status, the great suspension bridge at the Narrows now bears his name. It took 85 years until another famous explorer, Henry Hudson, arrived on the *Half Moon* in 1609. His vessel entered the river into what would be considered the harbor proper. Likewise, he too was rewarded for his efforts by eventually having that river named after him. The first European settlement in the area was established by the Dutch in 1624 on Governors Island, and it was followed in due course by another one in what we now know as Brooklyn. The Dutch called the tip of Manhattan Island Nieuw Amsterdam. It was part of the greater colony of New Netherland.

The period of Dutch control on the East Coast of North America began to decline in 1664 when England and Holland fought the first of three wars over this new-world colony. In November 1674, the Treaty of Westminster saw Holland cede New Netherland to the British. From that point forward, Manhattan Island became their premier port in the American colonies. Of course, all that came to an end with American independence. The port contributed to the new nation's prosperity and trade. With the Erie Canal, New York's port became a key interchange for domestic and overseas trade. Through the clipper ship era, South Street in Lower Manhattan became known as the street of ships. As early as 1838, steam began to supplant sail as a means of propulsion. The British flag *Sirius* was the first steamship to cross the Atlantic Ocean. In her wake followed many others, including the first Cunard Line paddle-wheel steamer *Britannia* in 1840, albeit from Liverpool to Boston, Massachusetts. The die had been cast, and, as with any technological innovation, the best was yet to come.

The term *liner* crept into the traveler's lexicon describing regular, advertised services by a ship to and from specific ports on a maritime timetable. In the 1850s, additional evolution in shipbuilding and design took place. Firstly, wooden hulls were replaced by iron hulls, and the paddle wheel gave way to the screw propeller. The Cunard liner *Andes* was the first to introduce this advance in 1852. Four years later, the same line introduced the *Persia*, a significantly larger vessel of 3,300 gross tons and 390 feet in length. A true behemoth, the *Great Eastern*, a five-funneled, six-masted paddle wheeler that also had a propeller, entered the transatlantic trade in June 1860.

After the Civil War, Cunard faced many rivals, including the American-flagged Collins Line. In the 1870s, more transatlantic steamship lines were formed. Preeminent operators were European, including the Hamburg-American Line, Holland-America Line, Inman Line, North German Lloyd, and the White Star Line. Oddly and unfortunately, American vessels were in the minority at this time.

America, long a magnet for people seeking new lives or fleeing religious persecution, became even more so for European immigrants. New York became the premier port of choice. In 1870, a department of docks was established to help cope with the torrent of passengers.

This period postcard gives a bird's-eye view of southern Manhattan, including the famed Battery with Castle Clinton at the tip. Very busy wharves and docks line the Hudson River on the left and the East River on the right.

One

THE GREAT

OCEAN BRIDGE

Of all the sea lanes in the world, the North Atlantic was the one with the greatest passenger traffic. In the beginning, ocean travel was anything but glamorous. Prior to the advent of steamships, sailing ships took over six weeks to cross. Apart from the peril of shipwreck, there was the constant threat of fire and deathly diseases. Births as well as deaths at sea became commonplace. Emigrant vessels were for some ship operators merely a vehicle for profit, and as little as possible was spent on food and decent accommodations.

National governments reacted slowly, and it often took significant disasters to get regulations changed. As the human tide of people seeking better lives beyond their native shores increased, competition for passage dollars caused gradual improvements to take hold.

The introduction of faster steamships cut the Atlantic crossing down to 14 days, and express liners did it in a week. What had been a little over 1.4 million immigrants crossing to America in the decade from 1830 to 1840 dramatically increased to over 5.2 million some 40 years later. It was the great ocean bridge, and the Statue of Liberty in New York Harbor was a beacon to the world. Even the staggering numbers above were small in comparison with the 8.2 million who took passage in the first decade of the 20th century.

As a result of increasing reliability, liner services colloquially became known as the Atlantic Ferry. Over its bounding course traveled millionaires, migrants, con artists, and countesses. In complete contrast to the steerage-class passengers, there were the very wealthy. For this caliber of individual, including American millionaires, the prestige of sailing on the fastest and largest steamers held great appeal. By the last decade of the 19th century, truly luxurious new liners, especially German, entered service. None were more breathtaking or amazing than the four-funneled express steamers of North German Lloyd and the Hamburg-American Line. They could cross in a week from Bremerhaven or Hamburg to New York. Entering service from 1897 to 1905, they were *Kronprinzessin Cecilie, Kronprinz Wilhelm, Kaiser Wilhelm Der Grosse, Deutschland,* and *Kaiser Wilhelm II.* This quintet, ranging from 14,349 to 19,360 tons, eclipsed anything afloat. That included the White Star Line's *Majestic, Teutonic,* and *Oceanic* as well as Cunard Line's *Campania* and *Lucania.*

Cunard Liner " Lucania "

The *Lucania* continued the evolution of the Cunard Line's passenger ships. Her maiden voyage from Liverpool to New York departed September 2, 1893. A sizeable liner of her time, at 12,950 gross tons and 620 feet long, she carried 2,000 passengers. In 1909, *Lucania* caught fire while docked in Liverpool and was declared a total loss.

AMERICAN LINER "NEW YORK."

The *New York* was one of the finest liners of the 19th century. At 10,499 gross tons and 528 feet long, she was also one of the largest and fastest. Entering service in 1888 for the American Line, the ship was originally named *City of New York* and flew the British flag. The postcard image shows her underway on the Hudson River after she had subsequently obtained US registry.

AMERICAN LINE
NEW YORK AND SOUTHAMPTON.

S.S. PHILADELPHIA
ARRIVING AT NEW YORK.

The *Philadelphia*, sister ship of the *New York*, was launched on October 23, 1888, as the *City of Paris*. She too was transferred to American registry. Both vessels operated on the express service from Liverpool, subsequently Southampton, to New York until being sold in 1920.

An evocative period postcard shows a transatlantic liner outward bound on a balmy and moonlit night. All the iconic images of New York's harbor are there to see, including the Statue of Liberty, several ferries, the Brooklyn Bridge, and of course, the magical skyline all lit up.

S/S Hellig Olav. Kobenhavn — New York.

The *Hellig Olav* was a 10,000-ton liner of Denmark's Scandinavian America Line. She entered service in 1902 and had a passenger capacity of 1,083. Although not in the class of the express liners of the day, the ship nonetheless appealed to Nordic emigrants. The company operated transatlantic service until 1935.

The *Kaiser Wilhelm II*, third in a series of crack North German Lloyd Atlantic liners, entered service in 1903. The ship was among the largest liners afloat at 19,361 gross tons and 707 feet long, accommodating over 1,880 passengers. The *Kaiser Wilhelm II* was seized by the US government at the onset of World War I. The ship survived the hostilities, and she was put in the reserve fleet until scrapping in 1940.

The interiors of the late 19th-century liners had significantly evolved and were now quite palatial. Typical of the onboard ambience was the Vienna Café aboard the *Kaiser Wilhelm II*. First-class passengers enjoyed a spacious environment in which to relax, converse, read, play cards, or enjoy coffee and pastries. Elaborately decorated ceilings and fine window treatment rivaled that of the finest hotels ashore.

AMERICAN LINE U.S. MAIL STEAMER "ST. LOUIS" (11,629 TONS).

In 1895, the American Line introduced two new liners—the *St. Louis* and *St. Paul*. They were 11,629 gross tons and 554 feet long. The *St. Louis*, illustrated here, established new standards of oceangoing comfort for American travelers. In 1925, the company ceased operating.

Hamburg-American Line introduced its *Deutschland* in 1900. At 16,502 gross tons and 684 feet long, she carried over 2,000 passengers on the run from Cuxhaven to Hoboken, New Jersey. In 1911, she was painted white and restyled as the cruise liner *Victoria Luise*. Finally, the ship was scrapped in 1925.

14

North German Lloyd's *Konigin Luise* debuted in 1897 at 10,785 gross tons and 544 feet in length. The ship's maiden voyage to Hoboken departed on March 22, 1897, but she only sailed on the Atlantic Ocean during the summer. After World War I, she was part of the German reparations and went on to further service with a number of different firms.

Not all passenger ships using the New York went across the Atlantic Ocean. The Clyde Line operated an extensive passenger and freight service along the Eastern Seaboard. In 1901, its new passenger liner *Apache* entered service. She could accommodate 240 passengers and catered to those who preferred a more casual and relaxing ocean voyage to places like Charleston, South Carolina, and Jacksonville, Florida.

In 1898, the 12,800-ton *Pretoria* entered Hamburg-American Line's service. She was utilitarian and a slower ship, carrying significant amounts of cargo and passengers. First-class travelers enjoyed sumptuous meals and flawless service in an ornate two-deck-high dining salon. This image shows linen-covered tables set with china, wine bottles, napkins, and fine stemware.

Hamburg-Amerika Linie   Speisesalon

An Bord des Doppelschrauben-
Postdampfers "Pretoria"

den

Holland-America Line's *Noordam* sailed on her maiden voyage from Rotterdam to Hoboken, New Jersey, on May 1, 1902. She was a moderate-sized vessel of 12,528 tons and 565 feet long and carried 2,278 passengers. After sustaining some damage in World War I, the ship was laid up and did not resume service until 1919. This continued until her sale in 1927 and scrapping in 1928.

HOLLAND—AMERICA LINE.

T.S.S. NOORDAM. 12531 Tons Register. 22070 Tons Displacement.

Two

SEA GIANTS OF THE EDWARDIAN ERA

Six years into the Edwardian era, in 1907, the Cunard Line put into service Britain's famous express liners the *Lusitania* and *Mauretania*. It was felt that these 31,000-ton liners, capable of carrying over 2,100 passengers, could rival their German counterparts. The White Star Line planned an express trio of the 45,000-ton *Olympic* in 1911, the 46,329-ton *Titanic* in 1912, and the 48,158-ton *Britannic* in 1914. The *Britannic* never entered commercial service, becoming a war casualty. The French Line competed in April 1912 with its new 23,666-ton liner *France*. To accommodate the fleet of larger liners, New York's Chelsea Piers opened in 1910.

The Hamburg-American Line riposte was a three-ship fleet. The *Imperator*, at 52,117 tons and 919 feet in length, could carry over 4,500 passengers. She was the world's largest ship in June 1913. The following year, the 54,282-ton *Vaterland* debuted, and the last and largest was the 56,557-ton *Bismarck*, in 1914. The onset of World War I precluded her from entering service. In 1914, the last of the sea giants, the beautiful *Aquitania*, came into service. At over 47,000 tons, she served briefly before the war. What the sea giants had in common—apart from their size, speed, and large passenger capacity—was the ultimate in interior appointments, spacious suites, and palatial dining rooms.

A period brochure describes the *Aquitania* as follows:

> With a length of 901 feet, a breadth of 97 feet, a depth of 92 ½ feet to boat deck, and a gross tonnage of over 47,000 tons the Aquitania answers in supreme degree the requirements of safety, seaworthiness, luxury and comfort. In the passenger accommodation the special needs of all classes have been considered, and the immense proportions of the Aquitania have rendered provision upon a scale of magnitude and comprehensiveness unparalleled in the history of shipping.

Although somewhat overshadowed, moderate-sized passenger liners also entered service. Among the notable were Cunard's *Carpathia*, *Ivernia*, and *Saxonia*, Holland-America's *Nieuw Amsterdam* and *Rotterdam*, French Line *La Provence* and *Rochambeau*, Red Star's *Lapland*, and North German Lloyd's *Amerika*, *Berlin*, *George Washington*, and *Grosser Kurfurst*. Others included Hamburg-American's *Cincinnati*, *Cleveland*, *President Grant*, and *President Lincoln*. Ships were only as egalitarian and class conscious as the times in which they existed. World War I would of course change all of that.

The *Carpathia's* maiden voyage departed on May 5, 1903, from Liverpool and Queenstown to Boston. At 13,603 gross tons and 558 long, she accommodated a little over 1,700 passengers. *Carpathia's* place in history is assured by the role she played in rescuing survivors from the *Titanic* on April 15, 1912. She too met a tragic end when she was torpedoed and sank on July 17, 1918.

In 1905, the Cunard Line introduced the twin liners *Carmania* and *Caronia*. Both vessels were over 19,500 tons and 678 feet long, capable of carrying about 1,440 passengers. The *Caronia*, illustrated here, differed from her sister in that she was not powered by turbines. After World War I, she continued to operate until 1931 when she was laid up and sold for scrapping in 1932.

The *Ivernia* was plain compared to the glamorous liners of her day. Her maiden voyage from Liverpool to New York departed on April 14, 1900. At 14,278 gross tons and 600 feet long, she was built primarily with the emigrant trade in mind, accommodating 1,730 passengers. *Ivernia* was torpedoed on January 1, 1917, off Greece and sank.

The *Nieuw Amsterdam* took its name from the original Dutch settlement established at the southern tip of Manhattan Island. Her maiden voyage departed on April 7, 1906, from Rotterdam to Hoboken. The *Nieuw Amsterdam* was a substantial liner of 17,149 gross tons, 616 feet long, and accommodations for over 3,100 passengers. She remained in service until 1932, when she was scrapped.

Lusitania became a household name for both positive and negative reasons. She arrived in New York in September 1907 on her maiden voyage. Adding to her allure was the fact her initial speedy crossing took the Blue Riband away from the *Kaiser Wilhelm II*. At this time, the *Lusitania* was the world's largest liner at 30,396 gross tons, 790 feet in length, and capable of carrying 2,165 passengers. On May 7, 1915, the ship was torpedoed off the Irish coast with 1,198 fatalities, including 128 US citizens.

The *Mauretania* completed her maiden voyage two months after *Lusitania*. She captured the Blue Riband from her sister and held it for 22 years. After serving as a troopship, *Mauretania* resumed commercial service in June 1919 and became one of the most iconic liners of the period until retirement in 1935.

The Ocean Steamship Company of Savannah, Georgia, was commonly known as the Savannah Line. In 1907, its new 5,654-gross-ton *City of Savannah* entered the coastwise passenger service from Boston and New York to Savannah. While of modest size, she proudly flew the American flag and served the nation in both world wars. She was finally scrapped in 1947.

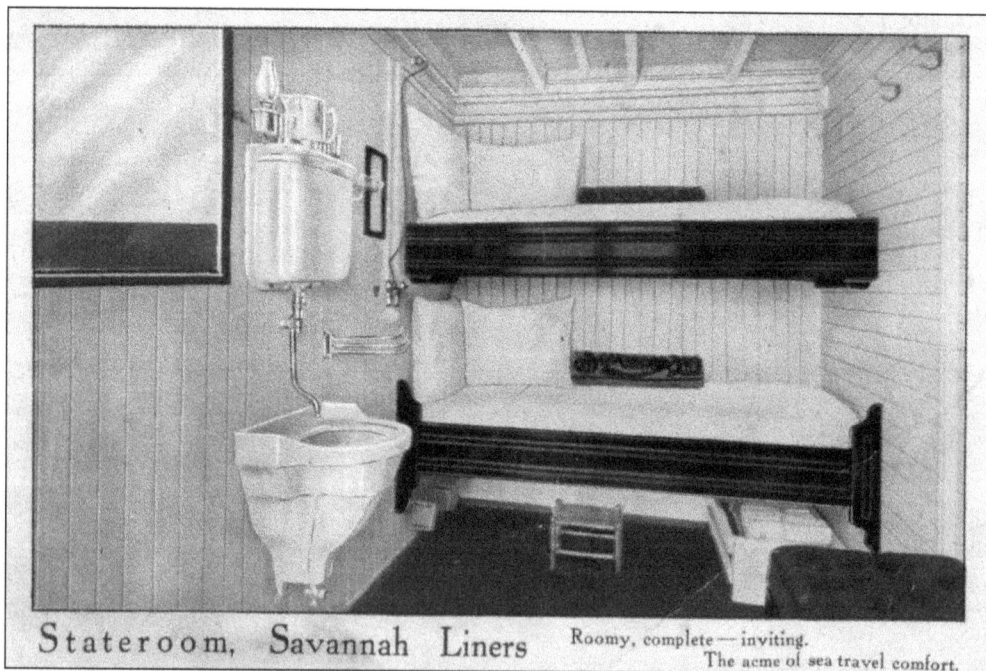

Stateroom, Savannah Liners   Roomy, complete — inviting. The acme of sea travel comfort.

The Savannah Line steamers were not in the same caliber as their North Atlantic counterparts, but they were comfortable nonetheless. This period postcard shows the interior of a typical stateroom albeit without toilet and shower, which was not uncommon. Those facilities were often down the corridor. Considering that the voyage was relatively short, it was not considered a great inconvenience.

In 1908, the *Rotterdam* became the new flagship of the Holland-America Line. She was among the larger transatlantic liners at 24,149 gross tons and 688 feet in length. Her passenger capacity was just shy of 1,200. During World War I she was laid up but resumed regular service in 1919. Retirement came in 1939 for this popular liner.

The *Rotterdam*'s first-class smoking room was, by the social mores of the time, a male bastion. It was here that business, a postprandial drink and cigar, or a game of cards might be enjoyed. All was possible within the surroundings of dark wood, columns, leaded stained glass, and comfortable banquette seating.

T.S.S. ROTTERDAM.   DINING ROOM.
24170 Tons Register.
37190 Tons Displacement.

In the grand style of the Edwardian era, the first-class dining room on the *Rotterdam* was built to impress. It followed the pattern of being two decks high, with an ornately carved ceiling with plenty of electric lights. The food was bountiful, quality excellent, and the service typified Dutch efficiency.

On this postcard, the *Rotterdam* is shown outbound in the Lower Bay, having just cleared the Battery. A plethora of harbor craft is included to capture the port's vibrancy.

T.S.S. ROTTERDAM. 24170 Tons Register. 37190 Tons Displacement.

HOLLAND-AMERICA LINE   ROTTERDAM - NEW YORK

12527 Tons Register.   "T.S.S. RIJNDAM."   22070 Tons Displacement.

The *Rijndam* was a sister ship of the *Noordam* and *Potsdam* and had the same general characteristics. The ship was laid up during the World War I after sustaining damage from a floating mine. In 1918, the United States acquired the *Rijndam* for use as a troop transport. But after the war's end, she was returned to her owners and operated until 1929.

T.S.S. NEW AMSTERDAM.

For some reason, on this postcard the Holland-America Line printed the name of its liner as *New Amsterdam*. In actuality, the name was shown on the ship's bow and stern as *Nieuw Amsterdam*. During her career, the ship enjoyed a good reputation and was of course spotless throughout. In fact, a marketing tagline, "the Spotless Fleet," was eventually used by Holland-America Line in the 1920s and 1930s.

New Docks Along West Street, South of Twenty-third Street, New York.

The Chelsea Piers opened in Manhattan in 1910 after eight years of construction. It was New York's goal to provide facilities of greater space and comfort for passengers. Driving this of course was the ever-increasing number of ships calling at the port and their increased size and passenger capacity. These piers remained in active service through the 1950s, supplementing Luxury Liner Row.

Cunard Line's *Carmania* was a sister ship of the *Caronia*, and they were similar from an exterior perspective. However, *Carmania* differed in that her propulsion system was three reciprocating steam turbines. During World War I, she distinguished herself by sinking the German armed raider *Cap Trafalgar* in August 1914. After the war, *Carmania* continued on the transatlantic route with some periodic winter cruising from New York to Havana, Cuba. In 1931, she was laid up, and scrapped the following year.

26

At the turn of the 20th century, North German Lloyd built three sister ships—*Main*, *Neckar*, and *Rhein*—all named after German rivers. The postcard illustrates *Main*, a vessel of 10,058 gross tons and 520 feet long, carrying 3,398 passengers. Her trade route was from Bremerhaven to Baltimore, Maryland, and Hoboken, New Jersey. The *Main* was ceded to Britain in 1919 as part of war reparations, ultimately ending up in France, where she was scrapped in 1925.

The *Cleveland* entered the transatlantic service of the Hamburg-American Line in 1909. She was considered a large liner of her day at 16,960 gross tons, 607 feet long, and accommodating 1,600 passengers. After World War I, she operated for several different companies, but the *Cleveland* was repurchased by her original owners in 1929. She was laid up in 1931 and scrapped in 1933. (Courtesy of the Steamship Historical Society of America.)

The Red Star Line's *Lapland* could be described as having the typical exterior of her time, with two funnels and four masts. New in 1909, she was average in size at 17,540 gross tons, 620 feet long, and a capacity for over 2,500 passengers. Her trade route was from Antwerp to New York. In the 1930s, she was transferred for a time to Mediterranean cruising from London. By 1933, a decision was made to scrap her. (Courtesy of Holland-America Line.)

The White Star Line competed by virtue of the size and comfort of its ships. Accordingly, the *Olympic*, first of a new class of three liners, entered service in June 1911. The *Olympic* was clearly elite at over 45,324 gross tons and 882 feet in length with a passenger capacity of 2,440. Her opulent interiors surpassed those of any other liner afloat and were comparable to baronial English manor houses. During World War I, the *Olympic* distinguished herself and went on to become one of the most popular liners of the postwar period. She was colloquially known as "Old Reliable" until her withdrawal from service in October 1935. However, she of course was best known as the sister ship of the ill-fated *Titanic*.

Although not mentioned by name, it is clearly *Olympic* that is illustrated in this postcard of New York Harbor at night. This is an impressive view showcasing the vastness of the Lower Bay. Poetic license was often taken inasmuch as the Statue of Liberty is shown but there is no hint of Manhattan or the Brooklyn Bridge in the distance. A tug with barges passes the starboard side of the dazzlingly illuminated *Olympic* nearing what is probably a Central of New Jersey Railroad excursion steamer.

Barely two weeks after the sinking of the *Titanic* in April 1912, the French Line introduced its new liner, *France*. More modest in size, the *France* was nonetheless substantial at 23,666 gross tons and 713 feet long with a service speed of 24 knots. Over 2,000 passengers were carried in surroundings evoking a French château and French Empire style. The cuisine, as one would expect, was without peer.

In 1913, the *Frederik VIII* entered service as the flagship of the Scandinavian America Line. At 11,580 gross tons and 544 feet in length, she was somewhat larger than running mate *Hellig Olav*. Her passenger capacity was 1,350, of which 950 was third class. The carrying of emigrants was the primary basis of *Frederik VIII*'s raison d'être.

A floating symbol of German nationalism was exactly what *Imperator* became on her maiden voyage departing on June 30, 1913. At 52,117 gross tons and 919 feet in length, she safely protected the claim of being the world's largest liner. In terms of passenger capacity, she could carry well over 4,500. The *Imperator* was fast, with quadruple propellers enabling a speed of 23 knots. During World War I, the ship was laid up and afterwards ceded to Britain as reparation. She became Cunard Line's *Berengaria* and continued in that role for the next two decades, until scrapping in 1938. (Courtesy of the Steamship Historical Society of America.)

The second liner of the new German trio was the *Vaterland*. At 54,282 gross tons, 950 feet long, she had a service speed of 23 knots and could carry 3,897 passengers. In 1914, the ship was interned in New York, and she was seized three years later by the American government and operated as a troop transport during World War I. (Courtesy of Foto-Archiv Fuchs.)

The maiden arrival of Norwegian America Line's *Bergensfjord* in New York Harbor was on October 7, 1913. The ship was 11,015 gross tons and 530 feet long, had a service speed of 15 knots, and carried 1,000 passengers. *Bergensfjord* was one of the few liners that was able to continue transatlantic service during the World War I. After an uneventful career, the ship was laid up and sold in 1946, becoming Home Line's *Argentina*.

Cunard Line's *Aquitania* was perhaps the best looking of all the four-funneled ships. By virtue of her size, 45,647 gross tons and 901 feet long, as well as her sumptuous interiors, she was magnificent. The *Aquitania*'s maiden voyage from Liverpool to New York departed on May 30, 1914, and she sailed briefly until being called for government service. The postcard shows her regal procession up the Hudson River, dwarfing other harbor craft.

CUNARD R.M.S. AQUITANIA   Tonnage 45,650

This outstanding aerial view of the outward-bound *Aquitania* shows her fine lines as she passes the Statue of Liberty. She is surrounded by a number of warships and tugs in this evocative scene from a time long gone. (Courtesy of the Steamship Historical Society of America.)

Three

AFTER THE GREAT WAR

In the aftermath of World War I, the passenger fleets of the combatants were in ruins. By the 1920s, attention was once again given to rebuilding the transatlantic link. Returning to service were the *Aquitania, France, Olympic, Rotterdam, Mauretania,* and *Nieuw Amsterdam.* The victorious Allies took the remaining German fleet as war reparations, including the *Bismarck, Columbus, Imperator,* and *Vaterland.* First to be refitted in 1921 was Cunard's *Berengaria,* formerly the *Imperator.* The same year, the French Line debuted its fashionable *Paris.* In 1922, the White Star Line introduced the *Homeric* and *Majestic,* previously the *Columbus* and *Bismarck.* The former German liners *Reliance* and *Resolute* came out the same year but now operating for the United American Line.

It took until 1923 for the *Vaterland* to reemerge as United States Lines magnificent flagship *Leviathan.* That same year, North German Lloyd introduced a new 32,000-ton *Columbus.* Two new American laws negatively impacted shipping. The first, the Volstead Act in 1920, prohibited the sale of alcohol. The second was the passage of the Immigration Act in 1924, a quota system on immigration based on country of origin.

To offset the significant loss of immigrant traffic, there was a new push to attract a broader middle-class passenger. Such passengers placed greater emphasis on informality and cost-effectiveness. A new series of moderate-sized vessels were built. The Cunard Line introduced 11 new 20,000-ton liners. The Anchor Line followed with five intermediate liners. This concept caught on with other steamship firms. Swedish American Line brought out the *Drottningholm, Gripsholm,* and *Kungsholm.* Italian flag operators introduced successful new liners during the 1920s, including *Augustus, Conte Rosso, Conte Grande, Conte Verde, Giulio Cesare, Roma, Saturnia,* and *Vulcania.*

In June 1927, the French Line's 43,000-ton *Ile de France,* an art deco masterpiece, was placed in service. She was an instant sensation. In the fateful year 1929, two major new liners entered service: Holland-America's 29,511-ton *Statendam* and North German Lloyd's 50,000-ton super-liner *Bremen.* Against this backdrop of glamorous new liners, the Wall Street crash occurred on October 29, 1929.

The *Stavangerfjord* entered service in 1918 for the Norwegian America Line. She was 12,977 tons and 553 feet long, carrying 1,226 passengers between Norway, Denmark, and New York. After being interned by the Germans in World War II, she resumed commercial service in 1945. After 45 years in service, the *Stavangerfjord* was retired in December 1964 and scrapped.

In 1920, the Swedish American Line acquired the liner *Virginian*, built in 1906. Renamed *Drottningholm*, she was placed on the Gothenburg to New York run with her maiden voyage in June 1920. During World War II, *Drottningholm* functioned as a diplomatic and refugee ship. Commercial service resumed in March 1946 and lasted 23 months. She was sold to Home Lines, who operated her as the *Brasil*, sailing from Italy to South America.

The *American Legion* began operating for the Munson Line in 1926 on the company's New York to River Plate (Río de la Plata) service. She was one of a series of 16 class-535 standardized passenger ships built in the waning days of the World War I. The liner was approximately 13,712 gross tons and 535 feet long (hence the class name), and she carried 560 passengers. The *American Legion* served in World War II but was subsequently scrapped in 1948. (Courtesy of the Steamship Historical Society of America.)

Cunard Line received the *Imperator* as part of the German war reparations and restyled her as its *Berengaria* in 1921. In this role, she was part of Cunard's express service from New York to England and France. Of the major liners in service at the time, she was fairly popular. During the Great Depression, she followed the patterns of other liners by making cruises to bring in additional revenue. The *Berengaria* was retired in 1938.

A grouping of tugs helps with the undocking of the *Paris*, which has just vacated her pier. Although she was launched in 1916, World War I precluded her entry into service. Her maiden voyage departed on June 15, 1921. At 34,569 gross tons and 763 feet in length, the *Paris* was one of the larger liners of the postwar years. In 1929, while docked in Le Havre, France, there was a fire on the ship. She was out of service for about five months. A subsequent fire in April 1939, also in Le Havre, resulted in her total loss.

The interiors of the *Paris* were in the art nouveau style, representing a huge change from the previous heavily wooded and conservative designs. The first-class cabin deluxe shown in this postcard image is light and airy with fine ceiling and wall details.

Two ocean giants in port together—the FRANCE and PARIS

On some occasions, the *France* (left) and *Paris* (right) were in port together. In this view, they are berthed at the Chelsea Piers in Manhattan prior to their respective departures. (Courtesy of the Steamship Historical Society of America.)

The United States Lines' *America* was originally the Hamburg-American Line's *Amerika* of 1905. After US troopship service in 1921, she began operating under the American flag. For her time, she was considered large, at 21,329 gross tons, 687 feet long, and with a capacity for 1,933 passengers. The *America* also served as a troopship in World War II but was scrapped in 1956. (Courtesy of the Steamship Historical Society of America.)

North German Lloyd's *George Washington* was interned in 1914 by the US government and used as a troopship. Postwar, she was acquired by the United States Lines on the New York to Bremerhaven run. The ship was 23,788 gross tons and 722 feet long, able to carry over 2,900 passengers. An encore troopship role for the *George* came in 1942, lasting until she was withdrawn from service in 1947. (Courtesy of the Steamship Historical Society of America.)

Another of the 535-class passenger ships, the *President Roosevelt* operated for the United States Lines. In this role, she sailed between New York, Plymouth, Cherbourg, and Bremerhaven. During World War II, she was used as an Allied troopship and ultimately sold for scrap in 1946.

In 1922, the United American Lines acquired two former Hamburg-American Line vessels. The *Resolute* operated on the North Atlantic route between New York and Hamburg. This liner was 19,692 gross tons and 615 feet in length, and she accommodated a little over 1,000 passengers. By 1926, the *Resolute* and sister *Reliance* were reacquired by the Hamburg-American Line. In addition to Atlantic crossings, they became well known as cruise ships. In 1935, the *Resolute* was sold to Italian operators who renamed her *Lombardia*.

The *Reliance*'s history and specifications were similar to her sister *Resolute*. She too served as both a transatlantic liner and cruise ship. In the latter role, she was quite popular in the 1920s and 1930s. The *Reliance* caught fire in Hamburg in 1938 and was declared a total loss. (Courtesy of the Steamship Historical Society of America.)

The Holland-America Line's *Volendam* maiden voyage departed from Rotterdam on November 4, 1922. She was 15,434 gross tons, 576 feet long, and able to carry only 585 passengers. Although torpedoed in 1940, she was repaired and resumed commercial service after the war, lasting until November 1951. Her sister ship was the *Veendam*. (Courtesy of the Steamship Historical Society of America.)

The *Leviathan* started life in 1914 as Hamburg-America Line's *Vaterland*, but she was interned by the US government. She eventually was used as an Allied troopship and renamed *Leviathan*. In July 1923, she reemerged as the flagship of the United States Lines. This photograph shows her outward bound just past the Battery in Lower Manhattan. The *Leviathan* operated on the North Atlantic run from New York to France, England, and later Germany. In January 1938, this veteran of two national flags was sold for scrap.

The *Columbus* began operating for North German Lloyd in 1924. She was one of the largest German liners of her day at 32,581 gross tons and 775 feet long, with a passenger capacity of 1,724. Like other vessels, she made periodic cruises in addition to her transatlantic duties. In December 1939, the *Columbus* was off the Virginia coast sailing without passengers, when to avoid capture by a British cruiser she was scuttled and sank. (Courtesy of the Steamship Historical Society of America.)

The *Ile de France* was the French Line's art deco masterpiece and is shown docking in New York. A large liner of her day, she was 44,356 gross tons, 793 feet long, and capable of carrying 1,146 passengers. The *Ile* had great panache with her modern style, outstanding cuisine, and deft service. (Courtesy of the Steamship Historical Society of America.)

Four

SHIPS OF STATE

A global depression followed Wall Street's crash, creating financial problems for steamship lines. The United States Lines puts it this way in a brochure for its new *Washington*: "It took courage and faith to put a new ship into commission in 1932, but the splendid support which the traveling public has given the *Manhattan* has more than justified the commissioning of a sister ship, the *Washington*, this year."

The first half of the 1930s saw the introduction of primarily moderate-sized cabin-class ships. They included the 26,000-ton *Britannic* and *Georgic* in 1930, the 28,000-ton *Champlain* and *Manhattan* in 1931, and *Washington* in 1932. The ships crossed in eight days or less, and their interiors were stylish, service was deft, and cuisine excellent. Even with the Depression, a luxury market existed. In 1933, the *Monarch of Bermuda* and *Queen of Bermuda* became known as "the Millionaires Ships." For $200 round-trip, one could cruise to Bermuda in a suite.

If this decade was remembered as the zenith of passenger ship style, it was also a time when nationalism took to the seas. European powers competed in building the largest, fastest, and most luxurious liners. These ships of state were constructed despite economic realities—Italy being a prime example. In 1932, the Italian Line brought out two new 50,000-ton liners: the *Rex* and *Conte di Savoia*.

Ambitious plans for larger liners required additional piers. Seven new Manhattan piers stretched from West Forty-fourth Street to West Fifty-seventh Street. Home of the most glamorous liners, they were nicknamed "Luxury Liner Row." The French Line's stunning 82,799-ton flagship *Normandie* became symbolic of this new opulent age. With three raked funnels, a streamlined hull, and beautiful art deco interiors, *Normandie* was breathtaking. Her maiden New York arrival on June 3, 1935, was a tumultuous affair. On June 1, 1936, Cunard White Star Line's new 81,235-ton *Queen Mary* proudly arrived in New York. Also a three-funneled liner, her exterior and interior were more traditional. The *Queen Mary* remained more popular than the *Normandie* and usually sailed full. There were still comfortable moderate-sized liners entering service, including the 36,000-ton *Nieuw Amsterdam* in 1938 and the 35,655-ton *Mauretania* in 1939. That year would rival 1929 globally, but for different reasons.

Shown outbound on the Hudson River, the Swedish American liner *Kungsholm* entered service in November 1928. This new liner was a little over 20,000 gross tons, measured 609 feet in length, and could accommodate over 1,540 passengers. The US government seized the *Kungsholm* in January 1941 and operated her as a troop transport. At the end of 1947, she was returned to her owners, who in turn sold the ship to Home Lines. She was renamed *Italia*.

The *Statendam* was a beautiful three-funneled liner introduced by Holland-America Line in April 1929. A large ship, at 29,511 gross tons and 697 feet long, she could carry over 1,650 passengers across the Atlantic. In the off-season, the ship cruised. When the Germans bombed Rotterdam on May 11, 1940, the *Statendam* was struck, caught fire, and became a total loss.

Inbound and passing the Battery, North German Lloyd's *Bremen* entered service in July 1929. The ship was a superliner in every sense of the word at 51,731 tons, 938 feet long, and a with capacity of 2,230 passengers. She claimed title to the Blue Riband as a result of her swift maiden voyage. At the onset of World War II, the *Bremen* fled to Germany. In March 1941, a disgruntled crew member set her on fire, and the ship was declared a total loss.

In this photograph, the *Europa* is shown docking at Luxury Liner Row on the west side of Manhattan. She was the *Bremen*'s sister ship and entered service in March 1930. When America entered World War II, she was used as a troopship, awarded to France for war reparations in 1946, and renamed *Liberté*. (Courtesy of the Steamship Historical Society of America.)

The Ward Line's twin luxury liners *Morro Castle* and *Oriente* were colloquially known as the "Havana Ferries." On August 23, 1930, the *Morro Castle* started on her maiden voyage from New York to Cuba's tropical capital. She was a modest-sized liner at 11,520 gross tons and 531 feet in length and could carry 530 passengers. For those able to afford the trip in the early years of the Depression, it was a great escape. (Courtesy of the Steamship Historical Society of America.)

On the evening of September 8, 1934, the *Morro Castle* caught fire off the coast of New Jersey. She was returning from another cruise to Havana, the conflagration grew out of control, and the passengers and crew abandoned ship. Luckily, rescue ships came to her aid. Unfortunately, 133 died in this tragic fire aboard one of America's newest liners. The postcard image shows the *Morro Castle* the next morning, beached at Asbury Park, New Jersey, and irrevocably ruined.

Canadian Pacific's flagship 42,348-gross-ton *Empress of Britain* entered service in 1931 and was a superliner of her day. Her normal trade route was from England to Canada, but in winter she cruised out of New York. Her around-the-world cruises became legendary. In late October 1940, the *Empress of Britain* was attacked by German bombers near Ireland and subsequently torpedoed and sunk by a U-boat.

In 1932, the Grace Line introduced a quartet of new passenger liners for its intercoastal service from New York to California. The *Santa Rosa*, *Santa Paula*, *Santa Elena*, and *Santa Lucia* were modest at 9,135 gross tons and 508 feet in length, and they carried 225 passengers. The *Elena* and *Lucia* were casualties of World War II. Happily, her sisters resumed commercial service, but they were placed on a Caribbean routing until being sold in 1958.

French Line's beautiful *Champlain* is pictured here in 1932 being escorted to Pier 88 by a number of tugs. She was better than average size at 28,124 gross tons, 645 feet long, and accommodations for 1,000 passengers. Although well regarded on the run from Le Havre and Southampton to New York, she was also popular as a cruise ship. In June 1940, the *Champlain* struck a sea mine and sank.

This postcard shows the new United States Lines' *Manhattan* outward bound in 1932. The *Manhattan* was a substantive liner at 24,289 gross tons and 705 feet in length, with a capacity of 1,200 passengers. Her normal routing took her from New York to Cobh, Southampton, Le Havre, and Hamburg. During World War II, she served the Allied cause as a troopship. Afterwards, she was kept in reserve and scrapped in 1964.

The Italian Line introduced its 51,062-gross-ton *Rex* in September 1932. She was a ship of state as Mussolini intended. In March 1933, she took the Blue Riband away from the *Bremen* for the speediest Atlantic crossing. In October 1939, the *Rex* was laid up in Bari, Italy. The British Royal Air Force attacked the ship on September 8, 1944, sinking her.

Another Italian ship of state was the lovely *Conte di Savoia*, whose maiden voyage was in November 1932. She too was considered a superliner at 48,502 gross tons, 860 feet long, and with passenger capacity of 2,060 and a spacious a Lido deck. The *Conte di Savoia* continued to provide transatlantic service until spring 1940. She was attacked from the air near Venice in September 1943. Although she was not sunk, the cost of returning her to service after the war was prohibitive, and she was scrapped in 1950. (Courtesy of the Steamship Historical Society of America.)

The job of docking the *Normandie* was no cakewalk, as the photograph illustrates. Some 14 tugs are in various positions alongside her 1,030-foot length as they work to bring her safely alongside Pier 88 on Luxury Liner Row. This aerial view also shows the 79,280-gross-ton liner's expansive outdoor decks. (Courtesy of the Steamship Historical Society of America.)

First-class accommodations aboard the *Normandie* were magnificent, as this period postcard reveals. A deluxe apartment would outshine many available in the world's grandest hotels. In the middle of a global economic depression, to be able to travel in such style was available only for the wealthiest of individuals.

Britain's ultimate ship of state was the Cunard White Star liner *Queen Mary*. Her maiden arrival in New York on June 1, 1936, was the maritime event of the year. At 81,237 gross tons, 1,020 feet in length, and carrying 1,995 passengers, she was elite among the superliners of the period. She is shown berthed at Pier 90 on the famed Luxury Liner Row. Her exterior, while pleasing, had very little of the *Normandie*'s cutting-edge modernity. (Courtesy of the Steamship Historical Society of America.)

From an interior design perspective, the *Queen Mary* was contemporary but without the chic of her Gallic rival *Normandie*. To this point, the photograph of her first-class main lounge shows a two-deck, capacious room with elegant burnished wood, direct and indirect lighting, and intimate groupings of chairs, tables, and sofas.

The photograph shows a group of passengers in the tourist-class restaurant aboard the *Queen Mary*. Tourist class, while comfortable, was a simpler and more economical way to cross the Atlantic Ocean for people who might otherwise not be able to afford it. Despite lacking the glamour of the first-class restaurant, its tourist-class counterpart still offered unobtrusive service and wholesome food.

A timeless image, which many thought would last forever, shows the *Queen Mary* approaching the tip of Lower Manhattan. She is outbound on the Hudson River on yet another Atlantic crossing to Cherbourg and Southampton. The regularity of the arrivals and departures of the great liners was a fabric of New York's life. During World War II, the *Queen Mary* was a very valuable troopship, and she happily survived the conflict.

In June 1939, Cunard White Star Line's new *Mauretania* entered service between England, France, and New York. She was a substantial liner of 35,655 gross tons and 772 feet long, accommodating 1,169 passengers. Like her contemporaries, the *Mauretania* was requisitioned as a troopship during World War II and made globe-girdling voyages in that role.

The last of the ships of state prior to World War II was the beautiful 36,667-gross-ton *Nieuw Amsterdam*. Her maiden voyage from Rotterdam to Hoboken via Boulogne and Southampton departed on May 10, 1938. This postcard shows her proceeding up the Hudson River towards her berth in Hoboken, New Jersey.

Five

SAILING TO VICTORY

World War II, like the first, devastated shipping. The *Bremen* departed New York on August 29, 1939, two days before hostilities commenced. Britain, France, and their allies declared war on Germany on September 1, 1939. With people seeking to escape Europe, the safest way to cross was on a US-flagged liner. Even small American liners like the *Iroquois* and *Saint John* were diverted to carry the tide of travelers seeking westbound passage.

At the start of the conflict, Cunard had 18 liners available for wartime service. Once the United States became a combatant, American flag liners joined the war effort. The value of the *Queen Mary* and *Queen Elizabeth* was critical and incalculable. Cunarders carried over 4.4 million Allied troops worldwide. Of that number, the two *Queens* accounted for more than 1.5 million troops.

By spring 1940, the war in Europe intensified. The Italian Line continued transatlantic service until Italy entered the war in June. During this time, the American Export Lines remained trading to Mediterranean ports. In July 29, 1940, the United States Lines' new 33,500-ton flagship *America* arrived at New York, direct from the shipyard with neutrality markings. She could not be used for Atlantic crossings but cruised to neutral ports.

With the nation and great parts of the world at war, national magazines and newspapers reflected the somber realities. Censoring was in place, causing difficulty in knowing which specific ships were sunk. Advertisements from American steamship lines moved away from the glamour of vacationing at sea and visiting exciting ports. Instead, their advertisements emulated domestic railroads, tending to the stern task at hand until victory. Prewar images of white-hulled liners were replaced by those of gray-hulled troopships and men in uniform. Germany, Japan, and Italy lost almost all of their passenger ships in the conflict. The Allies had many ships sunk or otherwise destroyed. One of the greatest losses took place on February 9, 1942, at Manhattan's Pier 88 when the *Normandie*, being converted to the troopship USS *Lafayette*, caught fire. Unfortunately, the great liner became a total loss and was scrapped. Peace came in 1945, but many of the liners that used to call at New York were lost in the fog of war.

When World War II started on September 1, 1939, America was still at peace, and American merchant vessels carried neutrality markings. United States Lines' *Manhattan* is shown proceeding down the Hudson River with her name, her owner's name, and two national flags in great prominence on her hull.

The *America*, entering service in August 1940, was also a ship of state. A large vessel at 33,961 gross tons and 723 feet in length, she had a normal speed of 22.5 knots and could accommodate 1,046 passengers. The *America* could not be risked on the North Atlantic. Alternatively, she cruised from New York to California and neutral islands in the Caribbean and West Indies. The *America* is shown on the official United States Lines postcard preceding her entry into service.

In the winter of 1939, United States Lines' *President Roosevelt* was placed in service between New York and Bermuda. This link was vitally important to that British island, as British passenger ships had been conscripted for war service. This official United States Lines postcard shows the *President Roosevelt* with neutrality markings in Bermuda waters. The cost of a round-trip at that time started at $70.

In 1918, the 14,000-ton, 443-foot-long *Siboney* was operated by the Ward Line on its route from New York to Havana. She served in both World War I and II. She is pictured here at a New York pier sometime during World War II. In 1948, the *Siboney* was put in the federal reserve fleet and ultimately scrapped in 1957. (Courtesy of the Steamship Historical Society of America.)

The US hospital ship *Hope* was a purpose-built vessel of 6,000 gross tons. She entered service on August 15, 1944. Although primarily used in the Pacific theater, the *Hope* was part of a vast fleet. Allied hospital ships were common visitors to the Port of New York during the war years. The *Hope* was deactivated in 1946 and held in reserve status until scrapping in 1978.

The 1940 photograph shows the US Army transport *Republic* at a New York pier just prior to sailing. The 17,910-gross-ton ship debuted in 1924 as the Hamburg-American liner *President Grant*, operating in the company's transatlantic service. The ship served in both World War I and II. In 1946, she was laid up, and she was scrapped in 1952.

SUSAN B. ANTHONY - Ex SANTA CLARA
WORLD WAR II CASUALTY

HE knows...do you...

THAT—American steamship companies are conducting the greatest
water transport operations in history.

THAT—without such operations the military successes of our Armed
Forces would be impossible.

GRACE LINE

In 1930, the Grace Line's *Santa Clara* entered service between New York and Chile. She was a liner of 8,060 gross tons, 486 feet in length, and could carry 157 passengers. As with other American passenger liners, she was drafted for troopship service in World War II and renamed *Susan B. Anthony*. On June 7, 1944, she struck a sea mine off the Normandy coast and sank.

During World War II, numerous American steamship lines advertised the services of their ships for the Allied cause. Representative of these is a Grace Line advertisement that appeared in prominent periodicals of the day.

The troopship *General George M. Randall* was one of 11 P2-S2-R2 type troopships built during World War II. At 17,800 gross tons and 622 feet long, this series of vessels could accommodate up to 5,000 servicemen. The ship served in both World War II and the Korean War and was decommissioned in 1962.

U. S. Army Hospital Ship "Seminole"
Arrives at Port of Embarkation
Charleston, S. C.

Photo by U. S. Army Signal Corps

The postcard shows the US hospital ship *Seminole*. Previously, she operated in Clyde-Mallory Line's coastwise service from New York to Texas. The government chartered the *Seminole* in 1942, originally for troopship service out of New York. Plans changed, and she was based out of Charleston, South Carolina, as a hospital ship. After the war, she was laid up and sold for scrap in 1952.

Another example of American steamship line wartime advertisements is this one from *National Geographic* for the Matson Line. It highlights Matson's role in providing its fleet for the Allied cause as well as the company managing Liberty ships being built in American shipyards.

Moore-McCormack Lines trio of 20,526-gross-ton passenger liners to South America were a familiar sight in New York's harbor. The *Argentina*, *Brazil*, and *Uruguay* were originally built for the Panama Pacific Line. This mid-1940s photograph shows the *Argentina* still in government service, but her funnel is painted in the colors of Moore-McCormack Lines. In 1947, she resumed her South American cruising until her owners built two new liners in 1958.

Six

POSTWAR LINERS

Postwar shipbuilding was hampered by shortages of steel, labor, and the devastation of shipyards. Slowly, prewar liners reentered service. The highlight of 1946 occurred when the *Queen Elizabeth* arrived. Within two years, *Media*, *Parthia*, *Caronia*, and *Stockholm* debuted. On February 12, 1949, the *Queen of Bermuda* made her first postwar sailing, and *Oslofjord* entered service that year.

On August 17, 1950, the elegant *Liberté* arrived in New York. Furness Bermuda Line's yacht-like *Ocean Monarch* entered service in May 1951. The same year saw the introduction of the *Ryndam*, *Constitution*, and *Independence*. The year 1952 was especially auspicious, with the July introduction of the superliners *United States*, *Flandre*, and *Maasdam*. In 1953, the new *Andrea Doria* arrived, followed in 1954 by the *Cristoforo Colombo*. Also new in 1954 were Greek Line's *Olympia* and Swedish American's *Kungsholm*. The Zim Line introduced its twin liners *Israel* and *Zion* in 1956. That turned out to be a sad year, with the sinking of the *Andrea Doria*.

A Cunard Line period brochure describes the glamour of ship travel:

> The excitement begins . . . but already the ship is a living, breathing thing. Footsteps in the corridor . . . stewards answering questions . . . page boys delivering telegrams and flowers. This is sailing day . . . and more, exciting still, sailing time! The great ship moves imperceptibly away from the pier. Forests of hands afloat wave to forests of hands ashore. Last minute good-byes span the widening ribbon of water. The voyage has started. All over the ship, a glorious feeling of anticipation reigns, ahead lies a few precious days of carefree gaiety . . . you are crossing the Atlantic.

In 1959, the author's parents took him to Manhattan to visit the *Cristoforo Colombo*. He was awed with the magnificent contemporary interiors. The Italian language was in abundance, adding to the allure. He recalls hearing the maitre d' addressing his staff. He said: "Remember this is first class and everything must be *tutto posto*—everything in order!" There were people who had emigrated 30 years previously and were now making their first trip back to Italy, with plenty of hugs and tears at sailing time.

Additional new liners arrived in the decade, including the *Argentina*, *Bergensfjord*, *Brasil*, *Bremen*, *Hanseatic*, *Rotterdam*, *Santa Rosa*, *Santa Paula*, and *Statendam*. In 1958, Boeing's 707 jet entered transoceanic service with great fanfare.

The superliner *Queen Elizabeth*'s first peacetime voyage to New York commenced on October 16, 1946. She was 83,673 gross tons, 1,031 feet in length, carried 2,348 passengers, and boasted 14 decks and 35 public rooms. This postwar glamour liner lasted until 1968, when she was sold to become a floating attraction in Florida. That venture failed, and the *Queen Elizabeth* was sold to become a floating university in 1970. Renamed *Seawise University*, she was being reconditioned in Hong Kong when a fire broke out on January 9, 1972, ultimately causing her to become a total loss.

The first postwar ships constructed for the Cunard White Star Line were two passenger-cargo liners, Media and Parthia. These twins were 12,346 gross tons, 531 feet long, and carried 250 first class passengers only on the Liverpool to New York run. The Media's maiden voyage departed on August 20, 1947, and she remained in service until the fall of 1961, when she was sold to the Cogedar Line.

The Swedish American Line introduced its passenger-cargo liner *Stockholm* in February 1948 on the Gothenburg to New York run. The *Stockholm* was 12,396 gross tons, 525 feet in length, and accommodated 585 passengers. In addition to her Atlantic crossings, she also made some cruises. On the foggy night of July 25, 1956, the *Stockholm* collided with the *Andrea Doria* inbound to New York. In January 1960, the *Stockholm* was sold to East Germany, which operated her as a vacation ship.

In May 1948, the *Britannic* resumed peacetime service for the Cunard White Star Line. Her maiden voyage was originally in 1935, but she was requisitioned for duty in World War II. The *Britannic* was 27,778 gross tons, 712 feet long, and carried 993 passengers. Her primary route was from Liverpool to New York via Cobh. In November 1960, the *Britannic* was withdrawn from service and scrapped the following month.

Cunard White Star Line's *Caronia* was built as a dual-purpose Atlantic liner and cruise ship when she entered service in January 1949. She was 34,172 gross tons, 715 feet long, and had a passenger capacity of 932. The *Caronia* had a distinct hull coloring of three shades of green. Colloquially, she became known as the "Green Goddess." In November 1967, she made her last Cunard voyage and was sold the following year.

The reconditioned *Ile de France* resumed service in July 1949 after her wartime trooping duties. She now had only two funnels instead of the original three but in all other regards still had that same appealing luxury and style. The postwar career of this much-loved ship lasted until 1959, when she was scrapped.

In November 1949, the *Oslofjord* entered service on Norwegian America Line's route between Norway, Denmark, and New York. She was a good-looking liner of 16,923 gross tons, 577 feet in length, and with a capacity for 625 passengers. The *Oslofjord* also became well known for cruises from New York. In 1969, she was leased to Costa Cruises. In July 1970, she caught fire while in Costa's employ and became a total loss.

When the French Line debuted its *Liberté* in August 1950, she was beautifully transformed from the former *Europa*. Her interiors represented the best of French design. *Liberté* was the third-largest liner in the world at 51,839 gross tons and 937 feet long, with accommodations for 1,502 passengers. In December 1961, she was sold for scrapping, which took place the following June.

The *Constitution* entered service in 1951, four months after her sister *Independence*, on the route from New York to the Mediterranean. At 29,000 gross tons and 682 feet long, she could carry 1,000 passengers. Through their careers, both ships were very popular. In 1969, the *Constitution* and *Independence* were laid up and sold. In 1980, they became Hawaiʻi-based cruise ships.

The superliner *United States* is shown passing the Statue of Liberty sometime in the 1950s on another crossing to Europe. Her record-breaking maiden voyage on July 3, 1952, won her the Blue Riband for crossing in 3.5 days. The *United States* was the largest liner built in America, at 53,329 gross tons and 990 feet in length, with top speed at 33 knots and a passenger capacity of 1,928. In 1969, she was abruptly taken out of service and laid up in Norfolk, Virginia. On July 24, 1996, the *United States* was then laid up in Philadelphia, Pennsylvania, where she remains to the present day. Numerous plans to renovate her as a tourist attraction or hotel have not yet been successful.

The yacht-like *Flandre* was the smallest member of the French Line fleet when she first arrived in New York in July 1952. She was 20,477 gross tons, 600 feet long, and carried 1,028 passengers. The *Flandre* primarily sailed on the North Atlantic until reassignment to the West Indies run in 1965. The photograph shows a Moran tug repositioning her after undocking from Pier 88. In 1968, the *Flandre* was sold to Costa Line and in 1992 to Epirotiki Lines. She was destroyed in a fire while at Piraeus, Greece, on March 24, 1994.

Holland-America Line introduced *Ryndam* and *Maasdam* in 1951 and 1952. The postcard shows the *Maasdam* at sea nearing New York. Like her sister, she was a modest-sized vessel at 15,024 gross tons, 503 feet long, and carrying 875 passengers. Her maiden voyage from Rotterdam to New York departed on August 11, 1952. In December 1968, the *Maasdam* was sold to the Polish Ocean Lines, who in 1969 renamed her *Stefan Batory* for its Canada-Europe service.

The *Andrea Doria's* maiden voyage was in January 1953 from Genoa, Italy, to New York. Her statistics were impressive at 29,083 gross tons, 700 feet long, and 1,241 passengers. This postcard was issued by the Italian Line as part of its publicity campaign. The *Andrea Doria* was only three years old when she was struck by the *Stockholm* on July 25, 1956. She was fatally damaged and sank the next morning with a loss of 52 lives.

The 17,434-gross-ton *Olympia* was the first new ship constructed for the Greek Line. Her maiden voyage to New York was in October 1953. Until 1955, the *Olympia* operated on the New York to Bremerhaven route, and thereafter to the Mediterranean. Between 1974 and 1982, she was laid up, sailed as the *Caribe* from Florida, and resold in 1993 to become the *Regal Empress* sailing from New York.

The *Queen Frederica*, built in 1927, was a veteran when she began operating for the National Hellenic American Line in 1954. Since 1948, she had been Home Line's *Atlantic* and before that the Matson Line's *Matsonia*. Advertised as being 21,000 gross tons and 582 feet in length, the ship could accommodate 1,179. In January 1955, the primary route of the *Queen Frederica* was from New York to the Mediterranean. A decade later, she was sold to Chandris Lines, cruising from New York, Europe, and Australia.

The *Bergensfjord*, new in 1956, was 18,739 gross tons, 578 feet long, and could accommodate 877 passengers. In addition to her Scandinavian service, she also cruised from New York. She is pictured here outward bound sometime in the 1950s. In 1971, she became French Line's *DeGrasse*. Two years later, she was resold to a Singapore firm. She was damaged by fire in 1977 and laid up. In 1980, during refitting for another sale, she caught fire and became a total loss.

Seven

A SEA CHANGE FROM CROSSINGS TO CRUISING

The *Ile de France* was retired in 1958, followed by *Liberté* in 1961. Other transatlantic liners were subsequently withdrawn, including *Britannic, Stavangerfjord, America,* and *Mauretania*. Despite this, plans were under way for new liners, six of which would be ships of state. The first of those in June 1960 was the stylish 33,000-ton *Leonardo da Vinci*. On February 9, 1962, French Line's 66,348-ton *France* entered New York Harbor for the first time. At 1,035 feet long, she was now the longest liner in the world and accommodated over 1,900 passengers. French Line publicists were effusive in describing the *France:*

> The *France* is an $80 million dollar floating pleasure resort with elegant dining rooms. Whether you dine with the Captain in the Versailles, or the famous Chambord, or the intimate Louisiane . . . the feasts are the same . . . incredible. Four clubs, an afterhours bar, Cabaret De l'Atlantique, two pools, two gymnasiums, a Parisian boutique, and the largest theater on the high seas.

In April 1964, the Zim liner *Shalom* arrived in New York on her maiden voyage. May 1965 saw the debut of Italian Line's 45,911-ton *Michelangelo*, with *Raffaello* following in July. That year also saw the legendary *Oceanic* enter service. Concurrently, the jet continued to make significant inroads. Zim Lines ended transatlantic service to Israel and the Mediterranean in 1967. The Cunard Line saw the handwriting on the wall. The *Queen Mary's* final voyage was in September 1967, with *Caronia* following. Equally bad news was the end of the *Constitution* and *Independence* in 1968 followed by that of the *Queen Elizabeth*. The *Argentina, Brasil,* and *United States* were withdrawn in 1969. By the mid-1970s, Cunard was the only line regularly operating on the Atlantic from New York. What had always been a commonplace event in New York for generations was now suddenly gone. No longer would there be sailings of half a dozen ships on a given day for Europe or South America. Only a limited offering of cruises from New York would be available. More vacationers were opting for fly-sail cruises from Florida or Puerto Rico. New York's harbor, which once roared with maritime activity, was now reduced to a whisper.

The *Empress of Scotland* was a Canadian Pacific prewar liner built in 1930 as the *Empress of Japan*. She was 26,032 gross tons and 666 feet in length, with a passenger capacity of 1,173. Originally operating on a transpacific routing, she was renamed in 1942. Postwar Canadian Pacific ended its Pacific services, and the *Empress of Scotland* sailed from Canada to Britain. In winter, she cruised out of New York. The Hamburg-Atlantic Line acquired her in 1957, and she was renamed *Hanseatic*. (Courtesy of Canadian Pacific.)

Another prewar veteran was Furness Bermuda Line's *Queen of Bermuda*, which originally entered service in 1933. With her sister *Monarch of Bermuda* they were colloquially called the "Millionaires Ships." Each vessel was 22,552 tons, 590 feet long, and carried over 730 passengers. This evocative photograph shows the excitement of sailing day as the *Queen* departs from Manhattan's Pier 95. In 1966, Furness ended all passenger service.

In July 1955, the Cunard liner *Ivernia* arrived in Montréal, Canada, on her maiden voyage. She was one of a quartet of 22,000-gross-ton ships that were 608 feet long. In April 1963, the ship was converted for cruising and renamed *Franconia*. This arrangement became permanent in 1967, when she entered the Bermuda cruise service from New York. This photograph shows *Franconia* in the twilight of a summer afternoon outbound in New York's Upper Bay. She was retired in October 1971 and eventually sold to the Soviet Union.

The *Statendam*'s maiden voyage was in February 1957. She was a good-sized liner at 24,294 gross tons and 643 feet in length and carried 852 passengers. Initially, she served on the North Atlantic, but by 1966 was primarily doing cruises. In 1981, she was sold to Paquet Cruises, operating as the *Rhapsody*. A final sale to Regency Cruises took place in 1986, and she sailed as its *Regent Star* until 1995. (Courtesy of Holland-America Line.)

Hamburg-Atlantic Line's *Hanseatic* was the former *Empress of Scotland*. Her owners acquired her in 1957 for their new service between Hamburg and New York as well as cruising. This postcard shows the *Hanseatic* in mid-Hudson moments after departing her pier. An unfortunate fire while docked at New York in September 1966 resulted in the total loss of the ship.

Pictured here is Moore-McCormack Line's *Argentina* early in her career, approaching the Battery in Lower Manhattan. The *Argentina* and her sister *Brasil* debuted in 1958 for the long-haul voyage from New York to River Plate (Río de la Plata) ports on the east coast of South America. Each of the liners was 23,500 gross tons, 617 feet long, and carried 553 passengers. In September 1969, Moore-McCormack Lines ended all of its passenger service. (Courtesy of Moore-McCormack Lines.)

In 1958, Grace Line introduced two modern cruise liners, *Santa Rosa* and *Santa Paula*. These twins were modest-sized ships of 15,371 gross tons, 548 feet in length, and accommodated 300 passengers. In 1970, Grace Lines and Prudential Lines merged to form Prudential-Grace Lines. Pictured here is the *Santa Paula* in New York's Lower Bay wearing the new funnel colors. Unfortunately, that same year saw both ships removed from passenger service.

Few in 1936 would have recognized the longevity and transformation of Union Castle's passenger ship *Dunnottar Castle*. A modest liner of 15,000 gross tons and 560 feet in length, she accommodated 508 passengers from London to South and East Africa. In 1958, the ship was sold to Incres Lines and extensively rebuilt, becoming its cruise liner *Victoria*. She is pictured here inbound in New York's Lower Bay.

The fifth North German Lloyd ship to carry the name *Bremen* debuted in 1958. She was originally the *Pasteur*, built in 1939, operating from Bordeaux to South America. The *Bremen* was 32,360 gross tons, 697 feet long, and could carry 1,034 passengers. In addition to transatlantic sailings, she cruised during the winter season. In January 1972, she became the *Regina Magna*, operating for Chandris Cruises in European waters.

In 1959, Holland-America Line's new flagship, the 38,000-gross-ton *Rotterdam*, entered service. Although she operated on the transatlantic route, she also was designed for worldwide cruising. The photograph shows the *Rotterdam* having just cleared the Verrazano-Narrows Bridge inbound from a cruise to Nassau and Bermuda. In 1997, the *Rotterdam* was sold to Premier cruises, operating as their *Rembrandt*. (Courtesy of Holland-America Line.)

Good music and lively conversation made a memorable evening in the Ritz Carlton Nightclub on the *Rotterdam*. (Courtesy of Holland-America Line.)

The *Leonardo da Vinci* rests on the north side of Pier 84 in 1966, when she was painted white. Built to replace the *Andrea Doria*, she entered service in July 1960 and was 33,340 gross tons, 761 feet long, and accommodated 1,326 passengers. The primary assignment of the *Leonardo* was on New York to Genoa express service. However, she also cruised to the Caribbean, Africa, and even Hawai'i. In 1976, the Italian Line ended all transatlantic service. The *Leonardo da Vinci* was eventually used by other Italian flag operators, but she was destroyed by fire in July 1980. (Courtesy of Flying Camera.)

The spectacular *France* was a modern-day successor to the *Normandie* when she entered service in 1961. She was among the largest liners of her day at 66,348 gross tons, 1,035 feet long, and carrying 1,944 passengers. In addition to her Atlantic crossings, she also cruised from New York. Her last trip for the French Line was in September 1974. In 1980, Norwegian Caribbean Lines placed her in service from Miami, Florida, as its *Norway*. In this role, she lasted until May 2003.

The *Shalom* was the pride of Israel and the flagship of the Zim Lines on her debut in 1964. Statistically, she was 25,320 gross tons and 629 feet in length, with a passenger capacity of 1,090. The *Shalom* sailed between Haifa and New York and also made cruises. However, the market conditions were not optimal, and in 1967 she was sold to the German-Atlantic Line and renamed *Hanseatic*. Further sales occurred over the years to Home Lines, Royal Cruise Lines, and Regency Cruises.

In 1964, Greek Line acquired Canadian Pacific's *Empress of Britain*, which was sold due to the continuing decline in transatlantic passenger travel. The *Empress* became the *Queen Anna Maria* and was 25,516 gross tons and 640 feet long. She operated to the Mediterranean and also did cruises. In 1975, the *Queen Anna Maria* was sold to Miami-based Carnival Cruise Lines, which renamed her *Carnivale*.

Home Lines marketed its new *Oceanic* as the "ship of tomorrow" when she debuted in 1965. A substantive vessel of 39,241 tons and 774 feet in length, she carried 1,600. The author and his parents took the *Oceanic* on a cruise from New York to Nassau in 1966. Apart from her Bahamas route, she also made cruises to other destinations. In 1985, she was sold to Premier Cruise Line and renamed *Starship Oceanic*.

This postcard shows a summer day scene in the mid-1960s at New York's Luxury Liner Row with eight ships. From bottom to top are the *Independence*, *America*, *United States*, *Olympia*, aircraft carrier USS *Intrepid*, *Queen Elizabeth* docking, *Mauretania*, and *Sylvania*. Times have changed, and it would now be rare to have so many liners in port at the same time.

When new in October 1965, Norwegian America's *Sagafjord* represented the continuing trend of dual-purpose liners. This 24,000-gross-ton vessel, 620 feet long, could accommodate 789 on transatlantic sailings and 450 while cruising. In 1983, she was sold to Cunard Line but retained her name. She was sold again to Saga Cruises in 1997, becoming *Saga Rose* until her retirement.

The Italian Line still had hope for the future of transatlantic service when it debuted its twin superliners *Michelangelo* and *Raffaello* in 1965. Each of the sisters was 45,933 gross tons, 905 feet in length, and accommodated 1,775 passengers. The photograph shows the *Michelangelo* docked at Pier 90 while the *Raffaello* is arriving in July 1965 on her maiden voyage from Genoa. Italian Line withdrew the twins 10 years later and sold them to Iran. The *Raffaello* was sunk in February 1983, a casualty of the Iran-Iraq War.

This photograph of the *Michelangelo*'s first-class bar shows a stylish and modern venue with passengers enjoying post-dinner cocktails en route to Genoa.

In April 1966, the *Kungsholm* entered service for Swedish American Line as a dual-purpose liner. She was 26,677 gross tons, measured 660 feet long, accommodated 750 on transatlantic crossings, and carried 450 on cruises. This photograph shows her maiden arrival in New York. In 1975, she was sold to Flagship Cruises.

The contemporary dining room aboard the *Kungsholm* was the setting for the superb service and cuisine for which Swedish American Line was known. This was especially important to her high-end clientele on long and lavish cruises.

North German Lloyd revived the name *Europa* when it purchased the *Kungsholm* in 1965. The *Europa* was 21,514 tons, 600 feet long, and carried 777 passengers on the North Atlantic and 478 on cruises. She continued in this role until 1971, when North German Lloyd discontinued all transatlantic service. The *Europa* was sold to Costa Cruises in 1981 and operated until 1984, when she was scrapped.

The *Queen Elizabeth 2* became Cunard Line's flagship when she debuted in May 1969. Popularly called the QE2, it was thought she would be the last transatlantic ocean liner. A superliner at 65,863 gross tons, 963 feet in length, and with capacity for 2,005 passengers, she was designed for both Atlantic crossings and cruising. She is pictured here early in her career outbound on the start of another voyage. (Courtesy of Cunard Line.)

This photograph shows the Theatre Bar on the QE2, complete with a piano for show tunes. Unlike the original Cunard Line *Queens*, this new monarch barely made a nod to traditional décor and was much more modern. (Courtesy of Cunard Line.)

High up in the forward section aboard QE2 was the Look Out, an aptly named public room. Here, passengers would mingle for conversation, cocktails, and a panoramic view of the ocean. (Courtesy of Cunard Line.)

Flagship Cruises *Sea Venture* and *Island Venture* were designed specifically for cruising to Bermuda and other islands when they debuted in 1971 and 1972 respectively. The *Sea Venture* was an average-sized vessel of 19,904 gross tons, 550 feet in length, and with a passenger capacity of 750. She is pictured here on her maiden arrival in New York on May 27, 1971. In 1975, she was sold to P&O Cruises, which renamed her *Pacific Princess*. She became famous for her role in the television series *The Love Boat*. After several other owners, she was finally retired in 2012.

The *Cunard Ambassador* and sister *Cunard Adventurer*, modest cruise liners of 14,115 gross tons, were introduced in 1971–1972. The *Ambassador* is shown docked at Luxury Liner Row with *Amerikanis* behind and proceeding to her berth. Unfortunately, *Cunard Ambassador* burned in 1974 and never reentered passenger service. (Courtesy of Bob Coolidge.)

Holland-America's 23,395-gross-ton *Veendam* was acquired from Moore-McCormack Lines in 1972 and was the third to carry the name. The *Veendam* cruised regularly from Manhattan to Bermuda and other tropical ports. She is pictured here outward bound on another cruise. *Veendam* had a number of other owners after being sold in 1984. (Courtesy of Bob Coolidge.)

Pictured here is Luxury Liner Row in the early 1970s, with all three berths occupied. From bottom to top are *Statendam*, *Rotterdam*, *Oceanic*, *Michelangelo*, *Doric*, and *Sagafjord*.

A seasonal visitor to New York was Canadian Pacific's flagship *Empress of Canada*, new in 1961. Primarily operating on the Liverpool to Montréal route, this 27,284-gross-ton, 650-foot liner did winter cruises from Manhattan. She was the last of the White Empress fleet and in 1972 was sold to Carnival Cruises, where she operated out of Miami as the *Mardi Gras*. (Courtesy of Canadian Pacific.)

The official Canadian Pacific postcard shows the spacious and inviting tourist class Carleton Restaurant on its flagship *Empress of Canada*. (Courtesy of Canadian Pacific.)

Grace Line's *Santa Mercedes* is seen in the Upper Bay of New York's harbor. Together with sisters *Santas Magdalena, Maria,* and *Mariana,* it was delivered in 1963–1964 as a passenger-cargo liner with significant container capacity. Each vessel was 20,000 gross tons, 547 feet in length, and carried 125 passengers on the route to the west coast of South America. (Courtesy of Flying Camera and Grace Line.)

A very infrequent visitor was Costa's *Eugenio C.* She was built in 1961 and sailed between Genoa and the River Plate (Río de la Plata) ports. A substantive liner of 30,567 gross tons and 712 feet in length, she carried 1,636 passengers. Her first visit to New York was in 1978.

The beautiful *America* is shown passing the skyscrapers of Lower Manhattan outward bound for Europe sometime in the early 1960s. She was sold in 1964 to the Chandris Lines and became its around-the-world liner *Australis*. (Courtesy of United States Lines.)

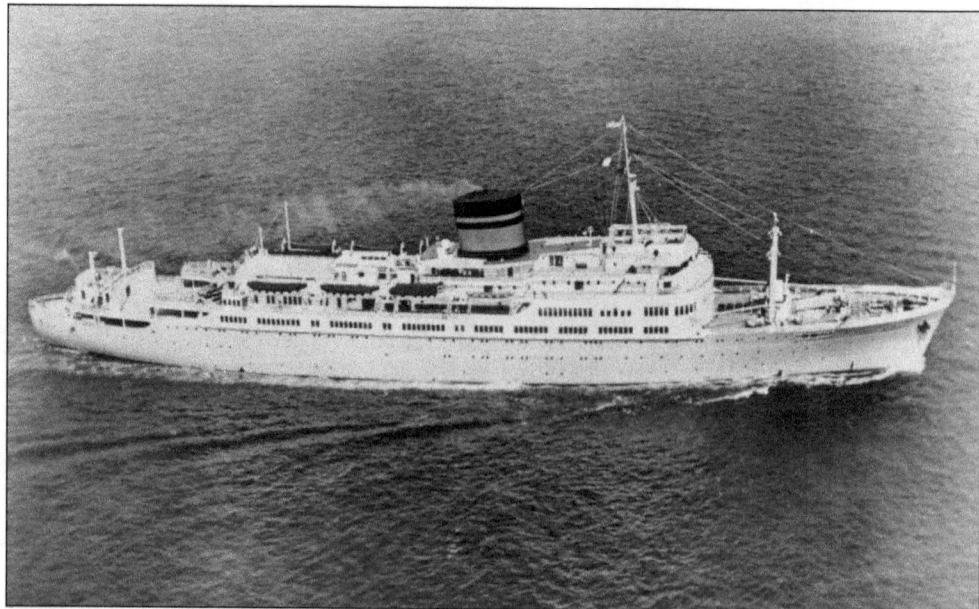

The 13,654-gross-ton *Ocean Monarch*, delivered in 1951, was a companion liner to the *Queen of Bermuda* and cruised to Bermuda and the West Indies. Because of the high costs of meeting new maritime safety laws, Furness Bermuda Line ended its passenger services in 1966.

CRUISING AND CROSSING...

s.s. ROTTERDAM tomorrow's ship... today!

Cruising and Crossing was the name of the brochure Holland-America put out to describe its flagship *Rotterdam*. From the onset, the ship would have to earn her keep on the North Atlantic as well as global cruising from the Caribbean to Alaska.

In 1960, the 20,067-gross-ton *Italia*, formerly Swedish American Line's *Kungsholm*, became totally dedicated to cruising by Home Line. She was colloquially known as the "Hostess of the Bahamas" because of her regular cruises from New York to Nassau. In 1964, the *Italia* was withdrawn from service and sold.

Home Line's *Doric*, originally the *Shalom*, was a full-time cruise ship. Sailing from both New York and Florida, she was a regular visitor to Luxury Liner Row on cruises to Bermuda and the Bahamas.

Chandris Lines *Amerikanis* started life in 1952 as the *Kenya Castle*, sailing from London to South Africa. This 19,377-gross-ton liner was 576 feet long with a capacity of 860 passengers. This artist's conception publicized *Amerikanis* prior to entering service. On May 20, 1968, she arrived in New York for her new owners. That summer, the author and two friends took one of her Bermuda cruises. After serving in different roles, the *Amerikanis* was scrapped in 2001.

Eight

MILLENNIAL LINERS

The last two decades of the 20th century saw surges in cruising popularity. New York was still a player but not the primary player—that title went to Miami. A few new companies eventually came to the port, including Bermuda Star Line, Regal Cruises, and Regent Cruises. Newer vessels were based in warm-weather ports. New York was also hampered by the ability of those older, slower ships to be able to reach destinations on a seven-day cruise. Typically, they were limited to the Bahamas, Bermuda, Canada, and New England. Luxury Liner Row was down to Piers 88, 90, and 92, rebranded as the New York Passenger Ship Terminal. Waterfront pundits wondered aloud how low the port would go.

In 1988, New York's fortunes improved with the establishment of Celebrity Cruises. Its *Meridian* and later the *Horizon* and *Zenith* sailed from Manhattan. Princess Cruises introduced its 70,000-ton *Crown Princess* to the market in 1990. By 1993, there were 16 ships representing 12 different cruise lines serving New York.

In the latter half of the 1990s, Carnival placed its 101,000-ton *Carnival Destiny* in New York. Periodic rotation of other Carnival ships followed. Concurrently, Norwegian Cruise Lines based its 91,500-ton *Norwegian Dawn* in Manhattan for Bermuda and Bahamas cruises. Other Norwegian ships also served the port. In 1996, Holland-America Line's *Veendam* entered service, followed in 1997 by its new *Rotterdam*.

The 21st century saw continuing evolution. In April 2004, Cunard Line's 151,000-ton *Queen Mary 2* made her debut. On May 14, the Cape Liberty Cruise Port, in Bayonne, New Jersey, became the seasonal base for *Voyager of the Seas* and *Empress of the Seas*. In 2005, Celebrity's *Constellation* and *Zenith* operated from there. Presently, *Celebrity Summit* is based there. Another change came in 2006 with the opening of Brooklyn's Red Hook Cruise Terminal. It became home base for the Cunard and Princess Cruises. Taken together with the facilities at Cape Liberty, four major cruise lines have left Luxury Liner Row. It is no wonder that Pier 92 is rarely used for passenger ships. However, a very positive development both for New York and Luxury Liner Row was the maiden arrival of the 144,000-ton *Norwegian Breakaway* in May 2013. She currently is the largest liner deployed year-round.

On May 8, 1980, the *Norway* debuted in New York, a port that previously knew her as the *France*. The photograph shows her approaching the Verrazano-Narrows Bridge. Her new role would be as the largest cruise liner in the world, sailing from Miami for Norwegian Caribbean Lines. (Courtesy of Bob Coolidge.)

The last cruise ship built for Home Lines was the *Homeric* in 1986—the second company vessel to carry that name. She was 42,092 gross tons and 669 feet long, with a capacity for 1,030 passengers. Two years later, Home Lines was acquired by the Holland-America Line, which renamed the ship *Westerdam*.

One of the few passenger-cargo liners to enter service in 1986 was Ivaran Lines *Americana*. The ship was 19,203 gross tons, 580 feet long, and accommodated 88 passengers on the New York to River Plate (Río de la Plata) ports. Subsequently, the ship began sailing from New Orleans, Lousiana, until withdrawn in 1999.

MEYER WERFT

Celebrity Cruises *Horizon* arrived in New York on her maiden voyage on May 12, 1990. A thoroughly contemporary ship, the *Horizon* is 46,811 gross tons, 681 feet in length, and can carry 1,798 passengers. The author took a Bermuda cruise on her in 2002. Three years later, the *Horizon* started one of her many transfers to other operators. (Courtesy of Meyer Werft.)

The 50,142-gross-ton *Asuka II* initially entered service in 1990 as the *Crystal Harmony*. In 1996, she reverted back to parent company NYK Line, serving in the Asia-Pacific market. The postcard shows *Asuka II* on one of her visits to New York on an extended cruise.

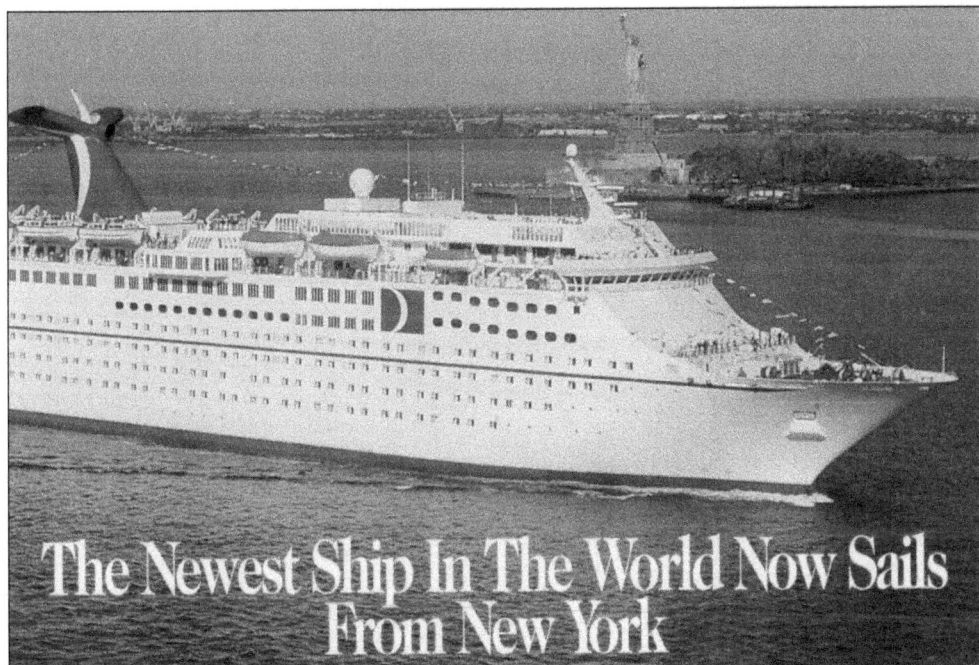

The Newest Ship In The World Now Sails From New York

The 70,367-gross-ton *Fascination* entered service for Carnival Cruises in 1994. For her initial summer season, she offered two-day weekend cruises to nowhere and five-day Canadian cruises from New York. The official Carnival postcard publicized her New York–based cruises. Subsequently, she joined her fleet mates sailing out of Miami, where she still remains in service.

Pictured here is the *Crystal Symphony* docked at the Brooklyn Cruise Terminal. She entered service in 1995 and is by today's standards a mid-sized ship at 51,044 gross tons, 781 feet long. The *Crystal Symphony* carries 922 passengers in luxurious style on worldwide itineraries. (Courtesy of Ian Fried–New York Economic Development Corporation.)

The sixth Holland-America liner to carry the name *Rotterdam* entered service in 1997. She is pictured here proceeding up the Hudson River towards her berth at the New York City Passenger Terminal. The *Rotterdam* is 62,000 gross tons, 778 feet long, and carries 1,316 passengers.

In 2001, the 92,250-gross-ton *Norwegian Dawn* entered service for Norwegian Cruise Line. Originally, she debuted the year before as the *Super Star Scorpio* for parent Star Cruises. The photograph shows the *Dawn* passing beneath the Verrazano-Narrows Bridge. (Courtesy of Ian Fried–New York Economic Development Corporation.)

Debuting in 2002, the *Carnival Legend* is a substantive liner of 88,500 gross tons and 963 feet in length. She can carry 2,056 passengers on her cruises. Before being based in Miami, the *Legend* initially served New York for a number of years. The photograph shows her outward bound on the Hudson River.

The *QE2* is shown departing New York. She is still cloaked in the pebble-gray hull color scheme dating to her post-Falklands refurbishment in June 1982. This was relatively short-lived, and it was repainted black in 1983. (Courtesy of Bob Coolidge.)

Back in her traditional Cunard livery, the photograph shows *QE2* in an evocative twilight departure from Manhattan. This image would certainly be after her 1986–1987 engine refit, at which time she also received a new wider funnel. (Courtesy of Ian Fried–New York Economic Development Corporation.)

One of the defining ships of the 21st century, the magnificent *Queen Mary 2* entered service in 2004. A dual-purpose liner, she is 150,000 gross tons and 1,132 feet long, with a passenger capacity of 2,620. The photograph shows her making an evening departure from Luxury Liner Row.

Queen Mary 2 now uses the Brooklyn Cruise Terminal in Red Hook. She has just left her berth and is now outbound on another Atlantic crossing. (Courtesy of Ian Fried–New York Economic Development Corporation.)

The beautiful and modern 93,530-gross -ton *Norwegian Gem* entered service in 2007. She cruises from New York to Florida, the Bahamas, and the Eastern Caribbean. (Courtesy of Norwegian Cruise Line.)

Holland-America Line's stylish 86,700-gross-ton *Nieuw Amsterdam* debuted in 2011, and the author took her maiden cruise from Venice down the Adriatic Sea to Greece. She is not a regular visitor to New York, but it is a treat when she does. The postcard shows her nearing the tip of the city to which her name pays tribute. (Courtesy of Holland-America Line.)

The expansion of Norwegian Cruise Line and its dedication to the Port of New York has no better manifestation than its mega-liner *Norwegian Breakaway*. This true resort at sea debuted in May 2013 and is 146,600 gross tons, and 1,062 feet long, with a passenger capacity of 4,028.

This contemporary view shows the truncated Luxury Liner Row in the 21st century. In this scene, two infrequent visitors are docked—the 44,500-gross-ton *Artania* of Phoenix Reisen and the 130,000-gross-ton art nouveau–styled *Disney Fantasy*. Here, *Artania* is on a cruise carrying European vacationers. (Courtesy of Byron Huart.)

The Yachts of Seabourn
INTIMATE SHIPS. UNCOMPROMISING LUXURY.

SEABOURN PRIDE · SEABOURN SPIRIT · SEABOURN LEGEND

Seabourn Cruises has used New York in the past. The company offers a high-end cruise product on smaller intimate ships such as the *Seabourn Pride, Seabourn Spirit,* and *Seabourn Legend.* The postcard gives an impression of the luxurious ambience and service

Holland-America's 86,273-ton *Eurodam* debuted in 2008 and is an occasional caller at New York. When she does visit, it typically is for Canada–New England cruises. Here, the *Eurodam* is outbound and nears the Battery at the start of a cruise on October 4, 2014. (Courtesy of Byron Huart.)

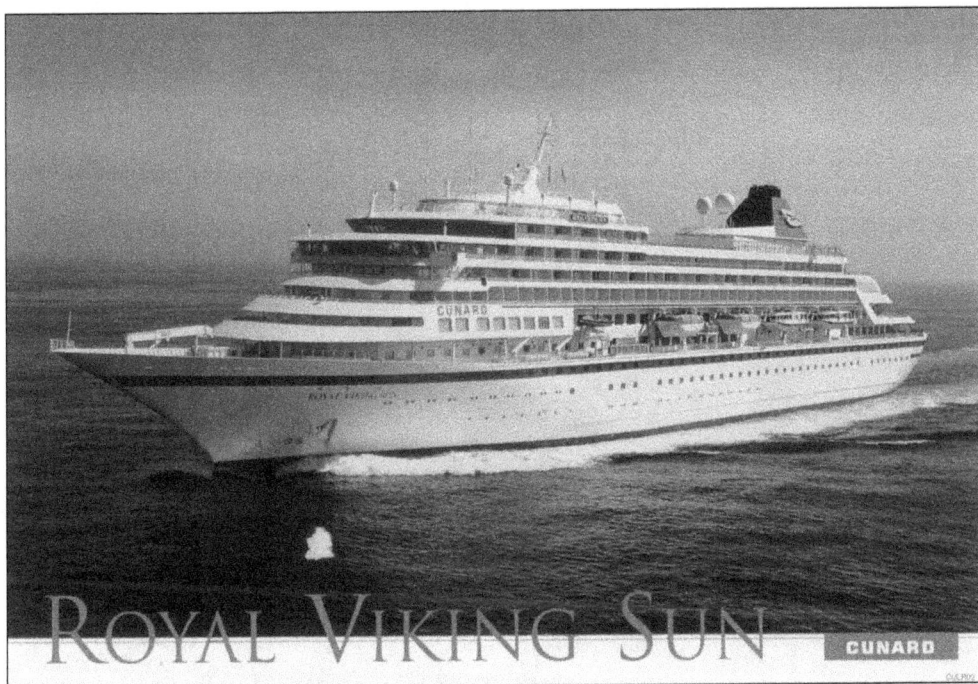

In 1988, Cunard introduced the luxurious 21,847-gross-ton *Royal Viking Sun*. She was formerly owned by Royal Viking Line. Periodically, she would sail from the Port of New York. The postcard shows her early in her Cunard career with modified funnel colors.

Another P&O liner, the 76,152-gross-ton *Aurora*, is home-ported in Southampton and only visits New York on occasion. However, she is scheduled to return in 2015. *Aurora* is shown outbound on the Hudson River approaching Lower Manhattan. (Courtesy of Byron Huart.)

The 69,203-gross-ton *AIDAluna* entered service in 2009. She is operated by Aida Cruises, a Carnival Corporation brand based in Germany. Primarily marketed to European travelers, she makes an occasional visit to New York. She is seen on one such recent trip in September 2014, docked at the New York Passenger Ship Terminal. (Courtesy of Byron Huart.)

Princess Cruises 113,561-gross-ton *Crown Princess* debuted in 2006 and is the second to carry that name. Normally, she sails from other American ports but has periodically cruised from New York. (Courtesy of Byron Huart.)

Hapag Lloyd's 8,378-gross-ton *Hanseatic* is 403 feet long and entered service in March 1993. Her 184 passengers enjoy a high class of cruising on worldwide itineraries. Very infrequently, *Hanseatic* is seen in New York.

The 57,092-gross-ton *Veendam* became the fourth Holland-America liner to carry the name, in 1996. Nowadays, she operates from California but for the past two years cruised seasonally from Boston to Bermuda. This photograph shows her earlier in her career when she was a more frequent visitor to Manhattan, departing from the Passenger Ship Terminal. (Courtesy of Byron Huart.)

The classic good looks of *Disney Magic* are apparent as she sails down the Hudson. In 2012, she did a series of cruises from New York. Here, the new One World Trade Center is still under construction. (Courtesy of Byron Huart.)

Princess Cruises 77,499-gross-ton *Sea Princess* debuted in December 1998. Not a frequent visitor to New York, she is however scheduled to be in the port in July 2015.

The ultra-luxurious *Seven Seas Voyager* is operated by Regent Seven Seas Cruises. She is 42,363 gross tons, 670 feet long, and accommodates 700 passengers. Her visits to New York are seasonal when sailing on Canada–New England itineraries. The photograph shows *Seven Seas Voyager* inbound to Manhattan. (Courtesy of Byron Huart.)

On September 27, 2014, there were five liners docked in New York, far from an everyday event. Pictured here, from left to right, are *AIDAluna, Carnival Splendor, Queen Mary 2,* and *Norwegian Gem* at Piers 88, 90, and 92. *Royal Princess,* not shown, was berthed at the Brooklyn Cruise Terminal. In the 1950s, this would not have been an unusual occurrence, but times have dramatically changed. (Courtesy of Byron Huart.)

The classy-looking *Balmoral* is shown on a recent port call entering the Upper Bay. She will return for another visit in September 2015. (Courtesy of Byron Huart.)

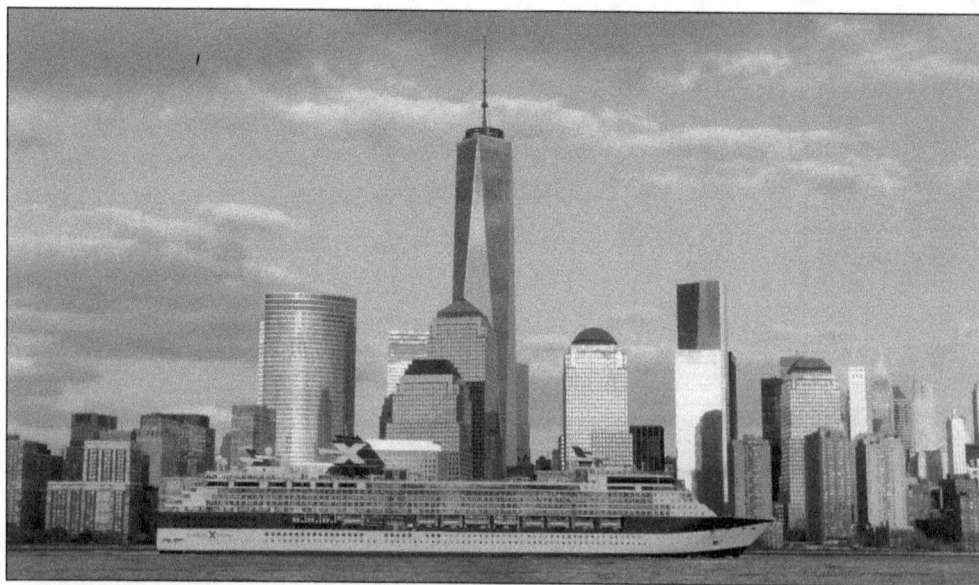

This view of *Celebrity Infinity* shows her sailing down the Hudson River with the now-completed One World Trade Center. The ship debuted in 2001 and is 91,000 gross tons, 965 feet long, and can carry 2,170 passengers. When operating in the Port of New York, the *Celebrity Infinity* is based at the Cape Liberty Cruise Port in New Jersey. (Courtesy of Byron Huart.)

This view of the New York Passenger Ship Terminal shows the *Azamara Journey* and *Balmoral*. Both of these vessels call infrequently, with the 34,000-gross-ton *Balmoral* based in Britain for Fred Olsen Lines. The 30,277-gross-ton *Azamara Journey* is operated by Azamara Club Cruises. (Courtesy of Byron Huart.)

Royal Caribbean's *Serenade of the Seas* usually sails from Miami. However, she will make a cruise from New York in October 2015. (Courtesy of Tina Rossell–Royal Caribbean International.)

Carnival Cruise Line's *Carnival Glory* has just departed her berth at the New York Passenger Ship Terminal. She is 110,000 gross tons and 952 feet in length, with a passenger capacity of 2,984. Carnival has rotated the ships for the New York market, and this photograph shows *Carnival Glory* proceeding downriver at the start of another cruise. (Courtesy of Byron Huart.)

The *Norwegian Gem* debuted in 2007, and she is 92,250 gross tons with a length of 965 feet. This photograph shows her docked at the New York Passenger Ship Terminal prior to departing on a Florida-Bahamas cruise. (Courtesy of Byron Huart.)

Nine

MEMORABILIA

It is easy to be nostalgic and wistful about New York and the passenger liners that served it. The port is exponentially quieter now than in the 19th and 20th centuries. This is not just limited to the diminished frequency of ship arrivals and departures. Only a handful of piers are used, primarily on the weekends, for cruise ship service. Corporate offices of global passenger lines, once numerous in Lower Manhattan, do not exist there anymore. They have followed the ships to Florida or California.

Filling the void, there has been a significant market in maritime ephemera, which brings one back to the time when New York was a city of ships. Before the advent of television, the Internet, or other media that people now take for granted, the marketing of steamship services was quite different. In the 19th century, handbills, newspaper advertisements, and flyers were used to spread the word about the arrivals and departures of ships. As ocean liners developed in size, scope, and luxuries, their publicity followed suit. Posters, brochures, and elaborate window displays with models of ships became common. Business at that time was still on a highly personal basis, so prospective passengers would make their reservations face-to-face with a steamship agent or by visiting a steamship line office directly. Once there, they would liberally be provided with sailing schedules, illustrated brochures on individual ships, deck plans, postcard images of the liners, pricing information, and baggage tags and luggage labels.

With the great diversity and number of steamship lines serving New York, as well as the vast number of ships in operation, the printed material available to prospective passengers was copious. Today, there are hard-copy cruise booklets available but in far fewer numbers than even the 1950s, and very few focus on a specific ship. Electronic brochures are downloadable from personal computers and are favored by some just as they prefer to download books.

In this chapter are illustrations of a few representative ship brochures from days gone by that ancestors perhaps might have picked up when making the trip of a lifetime across the sea so long ago.

This Eastern Steamship Lines rate schedule dates to 1941. It helped travelers select and price out their trip.

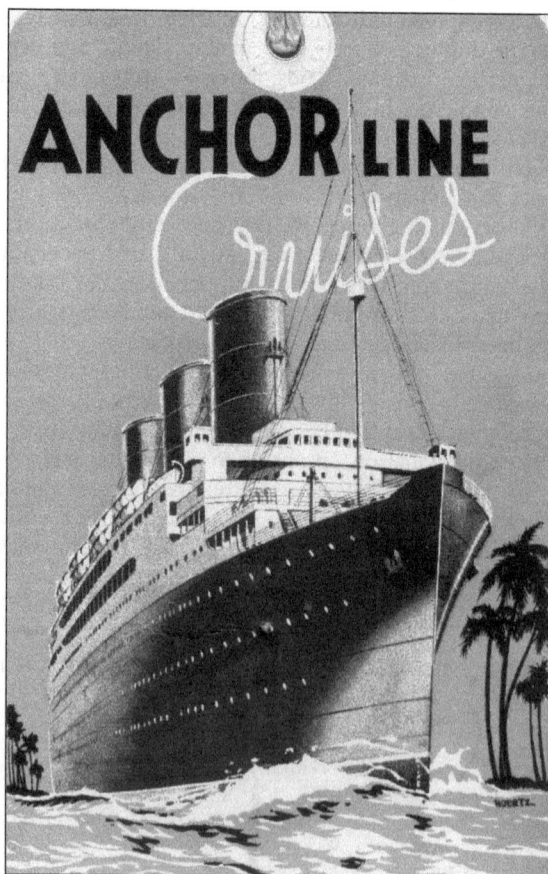

Baggage tags, such as this one from an Anchor Line 1927 cruise, served both a practical and marketing purpose.

The United States Lines took out full-page magazine advertisements, such as this one from 1932, announcing the introduction of its new transatlantic liner *Manhattan*.

From Broadway to Rio via American Republics Line appeared in numerous magazines in 1938.

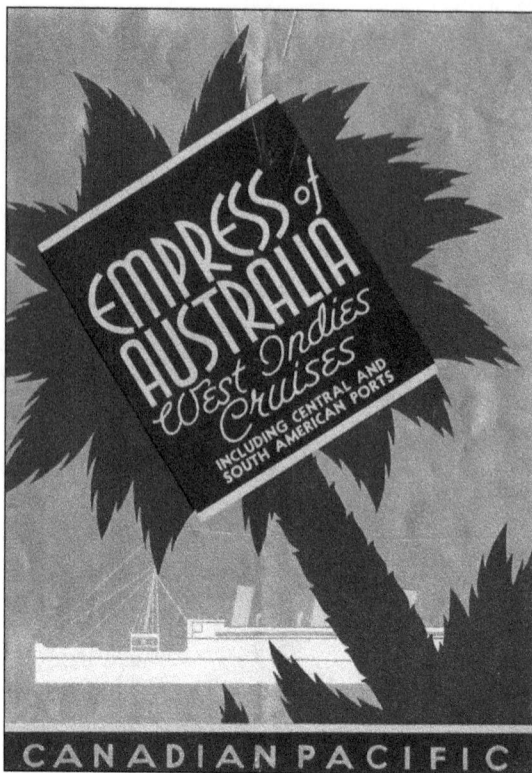

The cover of a 1920s *Empress of Australia* cruise brochure is both colorful and compelling.

This White Star Line leaflet advertises its various services in May 1907.

A 1936 Swedish American Line brochure features an illustration of its three liners.

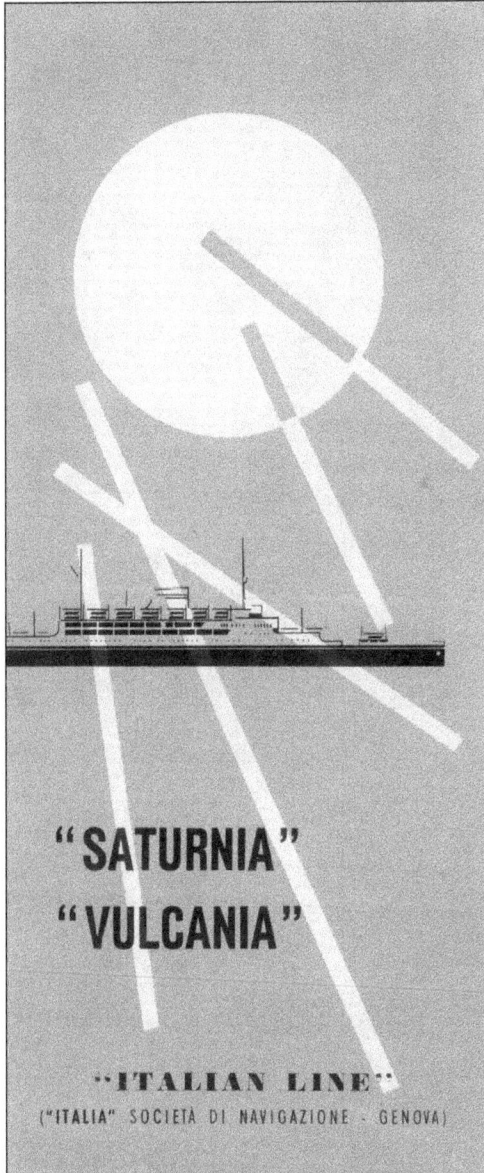

THIRD CLASS
THE SWEDISH WHITE FLEET

On THREE GREAT Liners

KUNGSHOLM   GRIPSHOLM
DROTTNINGHOLM

SWEDISH AMERICAN LINE

"SATURNIA"
"VULCANIA"

"ITALIAN LINE"
("ITALIA" SOCIETÀ DI NAVIGAZIONE - GENOVA)

An Italian Line brochure from the 1950s markets its *Saturnia* and *Vulcania*.

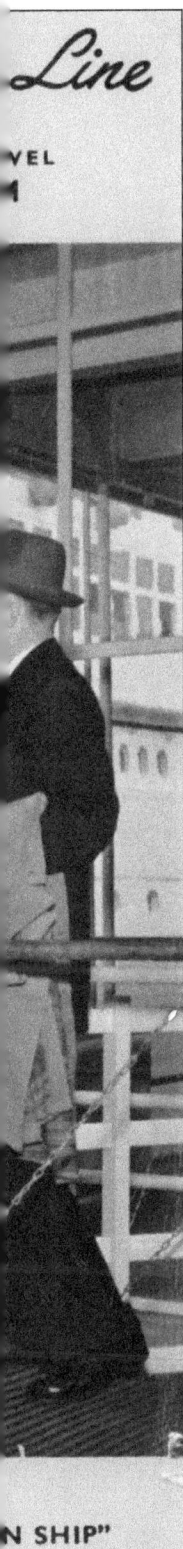

This Holland-America Line brochure from the 1960s reflects a bit
of glamour, depicting passengers embarking in New York.

German Atlantic Line's brochure advertises the maiden voyage of its new liner *Hamburg* in June 1969.

An elaborate maiden voyage brochure in 1983 heralds the introduction of the third liner to carry the name *Nieuw Amsterdam*.

A publicity brochure was issued in 1976 to market the New York City Passenger Ship Terminal—the last operating portion of Luxury Liner Row.

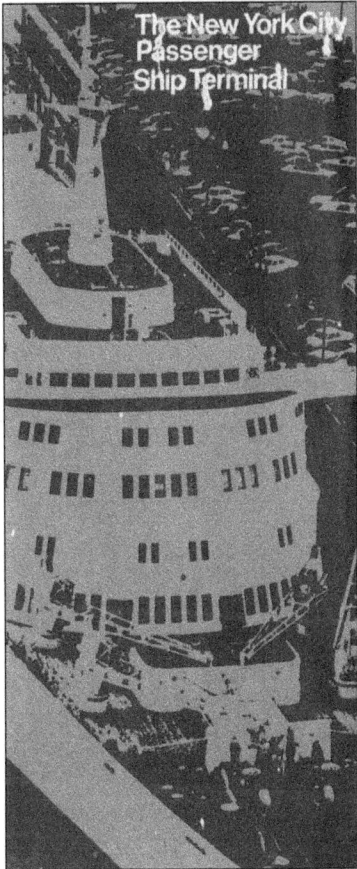

The New York City
Passenger
Ship Terminal

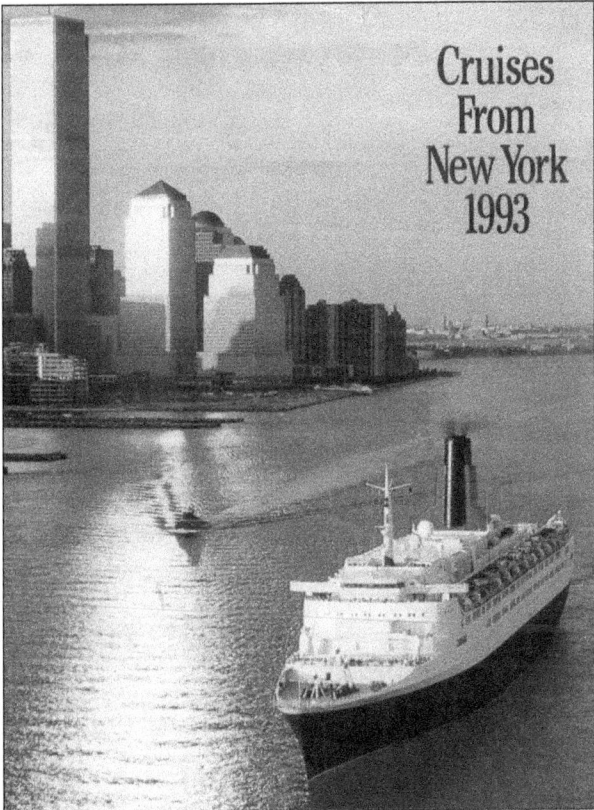

Cruises
From
New York
1993

The Port Authority of New York and New Jersey issued a brochure to publicize the 1993 cruise schedule for the 17 liners sailing from New York City.

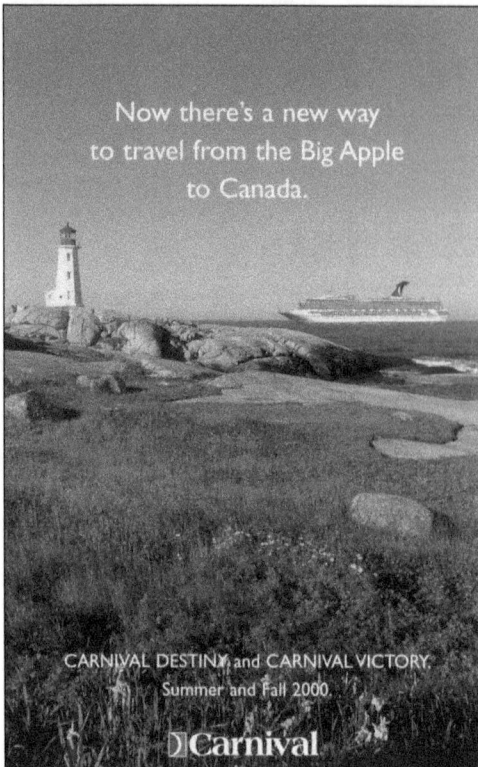

Carnival Cruises issued an advertising postcard in 2000 for its Canada cruises from New York.

In 2006, Princess Cruises issued a New York brochure for a series of Caribbean cruises on its new *Crown Princess*.

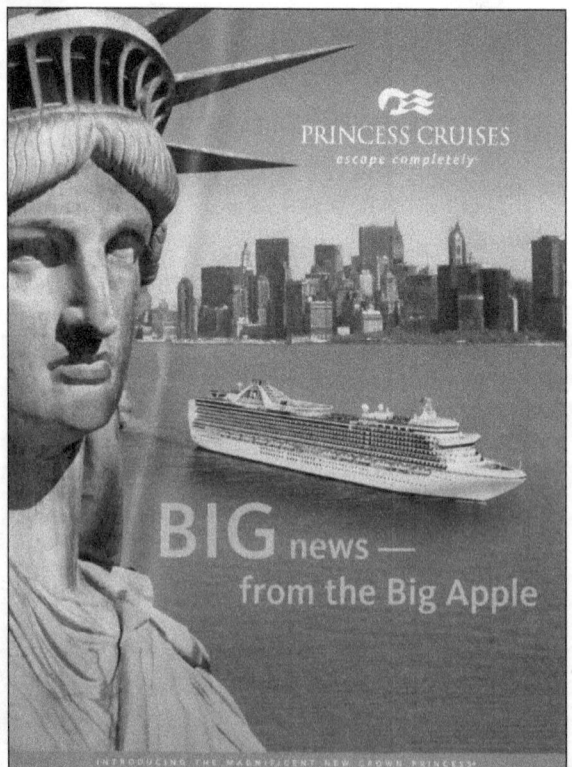

Ten

ON THE HORIZON

As of the time of writing in 2014, *Carnival Splendor* has been designated as a year-round New York–based cruise ship. Her itineraries have been enhanced to offer four- and five-day Canada cruises, seven-day Canada–New England cruises, and a program of eight-day Eastern Caribbean voyages between New York and San Juan, Puerto Rico. These are all in addition to the existing eight-day cruises to ports in the Caribbean, Bahamas, and Florida.

Royal Caribbean brought its giant 167,800-ton *Quantum of the Seas* to the Port of New York in November 2014 for a series of cruises. In 2015, the ship will then reposition to Shanghai, but her sister ship *Anthem of the Seas* will then take her place in the New York market.

Cunard's other two royal liners are infrequent visitors to the port. On January 18, 2015, the *Queen Elizabeth* sailed from Brooklyn's Cruise Terminal for a 43-day cruise to the South Pacific and Australia. Fleet mate *Queen Victoria* will sail from the same location on April 25, 2015, for an eight-day cruise to England. On July 25, 2015, Princess Cruise will send its *Sea Princess* down under for a 40-day Australia voyage.

Also through 2015, *Queen Mary 2* will offer transatlantic crossings interspersed with some seasonal cruising. Princess Cruises will offer Canadian and Caribbean cruises aboard its *Caribbean Princess* and *Regal Princess*. Through the remainder of the year, seasonal vacation voyages will be offered by Crystal Cruises, Holland-America Line, Seven Seas Cruises, and Silverseas Cruises.

Qualitatively, the Port of New York has improved, with the basing of several year-round mega-liners. Over the years, the variety of cruise destinations have also broadened to include not only transatlantic but also deeper excursions into the Caribbean, Canada, New England, South Pacific, Australasia, and even around the world. Cruise durations are no longer just limited to seven days or less. Aida Cruises, Asuka Cruises, Costa, Fred Olsen Cruises, Hapag Lloyd, MSC, P&O, and Phoenix are also calling at New York as part of their transoceanic voyages.

Quantum of the Seas will be the defining new liner cruising from New York starting in the fall of 2014. (Courtesy of Royal Caribbean International.)

Holland America's 55,575-gross-ton *Maasdam* will return to New York in October 2015 for a onetime call. She is pictured here inbound on a prior visit. (Courtesy of Byron Huart.)

The *Queen Mary 2* will continue to offer for years to come the only regularly scheduled transatlantic service from New York. She is shown here on an early-morning arrival on September 27, 2014. (Courtesy of Byron Huart.)

MSC DIVINA

MSC

The Italian cruise liner *MSC Divina* will be making a port call at New York in 2015. Normally, she is based in Miami sailing to the Caribbean.

Visit us at
arcadiapublishing.com

www.ingramcontent.com/pod-product-compliance
Lightning Source LLC
Chambersburg PA
CBHW050706110426
42813CB00007B/2100